THE WEB WIZARD'S GUIDE TO XML

CHERYL M. HUGHES

Boston San Francisco New York
London Toronto Sydney Tokyo Singapore Madrid
Mexico City Munich Paris Cape Town Hong Kong Montreal

Executive Editor: *Susan Hartman Sullivan*
Assistant Editor: *Emily Genaway*
Associate Managing Editor: *Pat Mahtani*
Executive Marketing Manager: *Michael Hirsch*
Production Supervision: *Diane Freed*
Cover and Interior Designer: *Leslie Haimes*
Composition: *Gillian Hall, The Aardvark Group*
Copyeditor: *Betsy Hardinger*
Proofreader: *Holly McLean-Aldis*
Cover Design: *Gina Hagen Kolenda*
Prepress and Manufacturing: *Caroline Fell*

Access the latest information about Addison-Wesley titles from our World Wide Web site: *http://www.aw.com/cs*

Library of Congress Cataloging-in-Publication Data
Hughes, Cheryl (Cheryl Marie)
The Web Wizard's guide to XML / Cheryl Hughes.
p. cm.
ISBN 0-201-76990-5
1. XML (Document markup language) I. Title.

QA76.76.H94 H84 2002
005.7'2--dc21 2002025587

12345678910—QWT—040302

TABLE OF CONTENTS

Preface ix

Chapter One **AN OVERVIEW OF XML** 1

What Is XML? 2

The Fundamentals of Markup Languages 2

The Beginning: SGML 4

HTML and the World Wide Web 5

An HTML Example 6

Enter XML: Why Is XML Needed? 9

The Benefits of XML 10

Separating Data from Presentation 10

Differences between XML and HTML 11

XHTML: The Best of Both Worlds 12

Creating Your First XML Document 13

Summary 17 ✩ *Online References 17* ✩
Review Questions 18 ✩ *Hands-On Exercises 18*

Chapter Two **A CLOSER LOOK AT XML DOCUMENTS** 19

XML Syntax 20

Components of XML Documents 20

The XML Declaration 20

XML Elements 21

XML Attributes 23

XML Entities 24

XML Comments 32

Well-Formed XML Documents 32

XML Parsers 35

Summary 36 ✩ *Online References 36* ✩
Review Questions 36 ✩ *Hands-On Exercises 37*

Chapter Three **DESCRIBING XML DOCUMENTS WITH DTDs AND XML SCHEMAS** 41

Using a Document Model: DTDs and Schemas 42

Using a Validating Parser 44

Overview of DTDs 48
Element Declarations 49
Attributes 54
Comments 58
External DTDs 59
Public DTDs 61
Using Both Internal and External DTDs 61
Overview of XML Schemas 61
Summary 63 ✧ Online References 63 ✧
Review Questions 64 ✧ Hands-On Exercises 64

Chapter Four ALL ABOUT STYLE: XML PRESENTATION 67
Creating the Presentation 68
The Benefits of Separating Content from Style 68
Using Cascading Style Sheets 68
CSS Syntax and Properties 69
CSS Rules Syntax 69
CSS Comments 70
CSS Properties 70
The Pros and Cons of CSS 78
Overview of XSL 79
Summary 80 ✧ Online References 80 ✧
Review Questions 81 ✧ Hands-On Exercises 81

Chapter Five NAMESPACES IN XML 83
What Is a Namespace? 84
Why Are Namespaces Needed in XML? 84
Using Namespaces to Avoid Confusion 85
XML Namespace Syntax 86
The Namespace Declaration 86
How to Determine the Scope of a Namespace 89
Example 1: Declaring a Default Namespace 90
Example 2: Declaring Two Default Namespaces 90
Example 3: Declaring a Default and a Prefixed Namespace . . . 91
Example 4: Out-of-Scope Example 91
Using Namespaces in XML Documents 93
Solution 1 93
Solution 2 94
Summary 95 ✧ Online References 95 ✧
Review Questions 96 ✧ Hands-On Exercises 96

Chapter Six LINKS IN XML 99
What Is a Link? **100**
Overview of Links in HTML **100**
The <a> Anchor Element 100
The <img> Image Element 103
Limitations of Linking in HTML 103
Links in XML **104**
Simple Links **104**
Simple Link Attributes 106
Defining a Simple Link in a DTD 109
Extended Links **111**
Defining an Extended Link in a DTD 112
Summary 114 ✧ *Online References 114* ✧
Review Questions 115 ✧ *Hands-On Exercises 115*

Chapter Seven NEW XML TECHNOLOGIES: XSL STYLE SHEETS AND XML SCHEMAS 117
The Importance of XSL Style Sheets and XML Schemas **118**
Overview of XSL Style Sheets **118**
XSL Formatting Objects (XSL-FO) 119
XSL Transformations (XSLT) 119
Overview of XML Schemas **127**
XML Schema Datatypes 128
XML Schema Occurrence Constraints 128
XML Schema Syntax 129
Summary 132 ✧ *Online References 132* ✧
Review Questions 133 ✧ *Hands-On Exercises 133*

Chapter Eight XML PROGRAMS AND PROGRAMMING 135
Programming with XML **136**
XML Parsers **136**
The Document Object Model **137**
An Example Using Microsoft's XMLDOM 138
The Simple Application Programming Interface for XML **142**
Comparing SAX and DOM **143**
When to Use SAX 143
When to Use DOM 143
XML and Programming Languages **144**
XML and Databases **144**
XML Query Language (XQuery) 145

A Sampling of XML Programs **145**
Distributed Authoring and Versioning on the World Wide Web (WebDAV) 145
Wireless Application Protocol (WAP) 146
Scalable Vector Graphics (SVG) 146
Open Financial Exchange (OFX) 146
Mathematical Markup Language (MathML) 146
Chemical Markup Language (CML) 146
Extensible Hypertext Markup Language (XHTML) 147
Resource Description Framework (RDF) 147
An Example: MathML **147**
The Future of XML **150**
Summary 151 ✧ *Online References 151* ✧
Review Questions 152 ✧ *Hands-On Exercises 153*

Appendix A: XML TOOLS AND RESOURCES 155

Appendix B: ANSWERS TO ODD-NUMBERED REVIEW QUESTIONS 159

Index 163

PREFACE

About Addison-Wesley's Web Wizard Series

The beauty of the Web is that, with a little effort, anyone can harness its power to create sophisticated Web sites. *Addison-Wesley's Web Wizard Series* helps readers master the Web by presenting a concise introduction to one important Internet topic or technology in each book. The books start from square one and assume no prior experience with the technology being covered. Mastering the Web doesn't come with a wave of a magic wand, but by studying these accessible, highly visual textbooks, readers will be well on their way.

The series is written by instructors familiar with the challenges beginners face when first learning the material. To this end, the Web Wizard books offer more than a cookbook approach: they emphasize principles and offer clear explanations, giving the reader a strong foundation of knowledge on which to build.

Numerous features highlight important points and aid in learning:

- ☆ Tips—important points to keep in mind
- ☆ Shortcuts—time-saving ideas
- ☆ Warnings—things to watch out for
- ☆ Review questions and hands-on exercises
- ☆ On-line references—Web sites to visit for more information

Supplements

Supplementary materials for the books, including updates, additional examples, and source code, are available at `http://www.aw.com/webwizard`. Also available for instructors adopting a book from the series are instructors' manuals, test banks, PowerPoint slides, and solutions. Please contact your sales representative for the instructor resources password.

About This Book

As the Internet continues to evolve, so do the technologies used to build Web sites and applications. Many of the original technologies, such as HTML and CGI, are being replaced with newer, more flexible, technologies to meet the never-ending demand for more functionality. Applications are becoming more sophisticated, requiring more integration among systems at a faster rate of speed. The Internet has also outgrown the Web as the only means to view these applications. In addition to the Web, the Internet clients of today include personal digital assistants (PDA's), cell phones, and pagers.

XML is one of these new technologies that will possibly re-invent the Internet as we know it! XML, and its related technologies, addresses the demands of new Internet applications by providing an extensible framework that is cross-platform and cross-vendor compatible. XML allows developers to create their own languages based on their needs and to pass this data between systems in a common format.

This book provides an introduction to XML and its related technologies. You will learn the fundamentals of XML syntax and how to create your own XML languages. You will also learn how to create document models for your XML languages and how to use style sheets to format your documents. This book is intended for beginners, but assumes that you at least are familiar with the HTML language the basic concepts of Web development. After reading this book you will have a solid understanding of XML and how it is being used.

Acknowledgments

This book is dedicated to my parents—Jean and Bill Hughes—and to my sister, Julie. I would like to thank my editors, Emily Genaway, Diane Freed, and Susan Hartman Sullivan, and all of the staff at Addison-Wesley for their support and hard work to make this book happen! In addition, I would like to thank my students at Harvard University for giving me inspiration and motivation, and Melanie for all of your patience and support. I would also like to extend my most sincere gratitude to the reviewers who offered many helpful suggestions during the editing process:

Michael E. Burt, Prince George's Community College
Locke Carter, Texas Tech University
GM Gehrig, Florida Community College at Jacksonville
Charles Hockersmith, University of Delaware
James Q. Jacobs, Central Arizona College & Mesa Community College
Andy Lang, Oral Roberts University
Hang Lau
Dr. Elizabeth Lane Lawley, Rochester Institute of Technology
Thom Luce, Ohio University
David Raney, Cuyamaca College
Hongchi Shi, University of Missouri–Columbia
Michael Weiss, Carleton University

Cheryl M. Hughes
May 2002

THE WEB WIZARD'S GUIDE TO XML

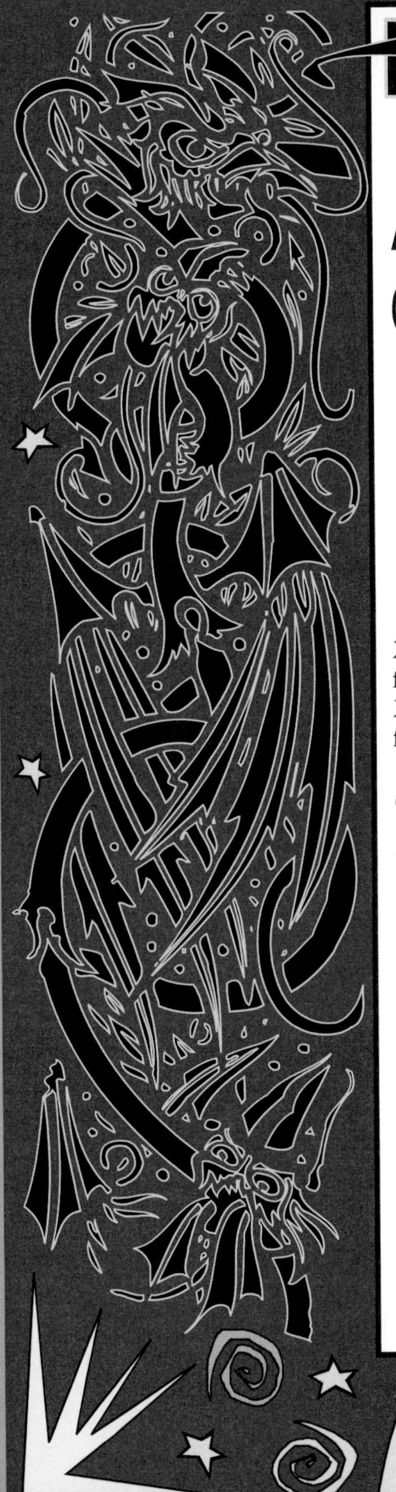

CHAPTER ONE

An Overview of XML

A free technology, XML allows you to create your own languages that are compatible with many different computer programs and operating systems. XML is ideal for Internet applications because of its standard format. In this chapter you will learn about the history of XML, how it is being used today, and its potential for the future.

Chapter Objectives

- To understand what XML is and why it was created
- To become acquainted with a brief history and comparison of markup languages
- To gain a brief introduction to XML
- To understand the differences between XML and HTML
- To discover the basics of XHTML
- To look briefly at the structure of an XML document

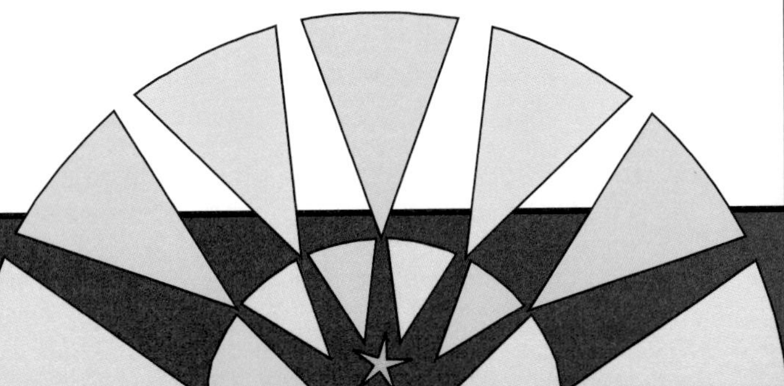

What Is XML?

XML, the Extensible Markup Language, is not in itself a markup language but rather a set of standardized tools that can be used to create new markup languages. XML can be more accurately defined as a **metalanguage**: a vocabulary consisting of **syntax** (language rules) and structure that offers a flexible, highly configurable means of defining custom elements for organizing and storing information that fit the needs of the data. Developers can use the XML specification to develop their own sets of markup elements based on the data the elements are meant to describe. Using XML, industries, companies, and individuals alike can create unique languages for defining their specific data. For example, MathML, Mathematical Markup Language, is one such XML vocabulary that was created for both describing and presenting mathematical data.

Like many Web technologies, XML is an open standard, meaning that it is not tied to any one operating system (like Windows, UNIX, or Macintosh) program, or vendor applications. This makes XML completely portable among various platforms and software programs. And because XML documents are plain text files, they can be created, viewed, and modified using any text editor, such as Notepad for Windows, SimpleText for Macintosh, or vi for UNIX systems.

☆**WARNING** XML was designed to produce **code** (special formatting instructions) that is readable by both machines and humans, so anyone with a text editor can open an XML document and look at the content. However, even though XML provides the flexibility to create markup elements that are meaningful to the content of the data, there are no rules that say tags must be developed this way.

The Fundamentals of Markup Languages

To understand XML, you need to understand the basics of markup languages and their use. A **markup language** is simply a set of rules that define the layout, format, or structure of text within a document. After markup instructions are added to a document, the document must then be **read**, or processed, by a program that knows how to interpret the markup elements.

Markup languages, and programs that format text based on special formatting instructions, have been in use for many years. For example, most computer users have used a word processing program, such as Microsoft Word or Corel WordPerfect, to create documents. These programs provide simple buttons and menus that are used to create formatting and styles within a document, and learning and using these programs is fairly easy. For example, using Word, if you want to make a certain section of the text bold, you highlight the desired text and click a button to make the text bold. Behind the scenes, certain proprietary symbols are applied to the section that tell the program how to display the data—in this case, bold type. This is illustrated in Figures 1.1 and 1.2.

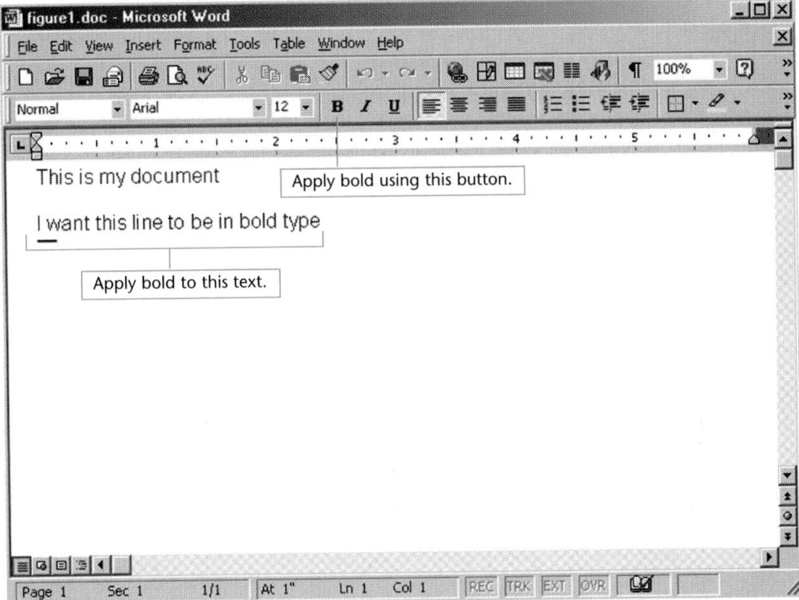

Figure 1.1 Word Document before Bold Style Is Applied

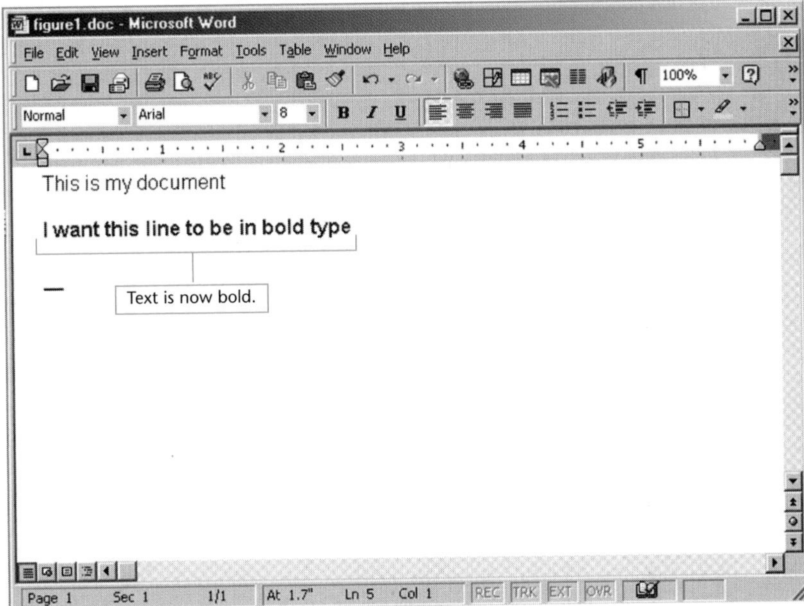

Figure 1.2 Word Document with Bold Style Applied

However, using a program such as Word is limiting because Word files can be viewed only by the Word program. The format for Word documents is **proprietary**, meaning that the format can be used only by one particular program. In addition, these documents are stored in a **binary** format, meaning that you cannot open and look at them using a plain text editor. This creates problems if you want to use another program or use a different platform to view or modify the document: The documents are not **portable** because they are tied to a particular piece of software, like the Microsoft Word, and, in some cases, to a particular operating system, such as Windows.

Word documents can, however, be converted to other formats using conversion programs, thereby allowing another program, such as WordPerfect, to open and view a document created in Word. But to do this, the underlying structure of the document must be changed to apply WordPerfect's proprietary styles and symbols to the document. As a result, the document may lose some formatting styles if the new program does not support them. After the conversion, the underlying structure of the document has been changed to the format for the new program, and it can no longer be read by the old one.

The need to standardize document formatting was realized many decades ago, and work began in the 1960s to develop a standardized document markup language that would be independent of a specific platform and program. SGML (the Standard Generalized Markup Language), the first such standardized markup language, gained moderate acceptance. But it wasn't until the World Wide Web and HTML (Hypertext Markup Language) took the world by storm in the mid-1990s that the benefits of such an open standard for markup languages became overwhelmingly apparent. SGML and HTML are discussed later in this chapter.

The HTML specification provides **content developers** (people who create documents and other information to be displayed on the Internet) with a portable document format that is not tied to any particular program or platform. And because HTML is an open standard, it costs nothing to use. HTML documents, like XML documents, are plain text files that can be created, viewed, and modified using any text editor. This gives developers a great deal of flexibility and allows them to move files freely among platforms and programs. For example, an HTML file created with a Macintosh text editor would look the same when opened in a Windows text editor, and it would be displayed the same when viewed using a **Web browser**—a program, such as Netscape Navigator or Internet Explorer, that is used to navigate the Internet—either on a Macintosh or a Windows computer.

The Beginning: SGML

SGML is the ancestor of, and provides the framework for, both XML and HTML. SGML was developed to create markup languages for large documents, such as technical documentation. It was adopted as an international standard by the ISO, the International Organization for Standardization, in 1986, and has been widely used by many industries—including the automotive industry, health care, the Internal Revenue Service, and the U.S. Department of Defense—for large-scale documentation projects. SGML's primary strength lies in providing a standard format and structure for large documents, thereby allowing them to be used by a number of programs.

Like XML, SGML provides a framework for creating other languages. However, SGML is extremely complex, making it expensive to develop software to process the code. SGML has proved useful mainly to corporations and other organizations that have the expertise and budget to implement the expansive SGML specification. Because of these constraints, it has not gained wide acceptance in the marketplace for small or medium-sized projects.

When the World Wide Web was first being created in the late 1980s and early 1990s, SGML was employed as the perfect tool to build the markup language that would be used to create documents for this new medium of information exchange. HTML was developed as a lightweight SGML language by researchers at CERN, the European Organization for Nuclear Research, in the early 1990s. CERN had been involved in working on the SGML specification for many years. HTML was much smaller than SGML and gained widespread acceptance very quickly. HTML was adopted shortly thereafter by the World Wide Web Consortium (W3C), the organization that creates standards for Internet technologies. The W3C continues to maintain the HTML specification, currently at version 4.01.

HTML and the World Wide Web

HTML made its debut in the mid-1990s as the markup language used to create pages to be viewed on the World Wide Web using a Web browser. HTML was developed as an open standard, meaning that it is free to use and is not tied to any particular vendor; there is no need to purchase licenses in order to use HTML. Because HTML is smaller than SGML, it is fairly easy to learn the syntax and also to write programs to interpret the markup, such as a Web browser. Because HTML documents are simple text documents with markup elements embedded in the text, they are completely portable among platforms and programs. HTML documents can be displayed using any program running on any operating system that knows how to interpret HTML. This portability was a revolutionary idea, and it has greatly contributed to the overwhelming success of the World Wide Web over the past decade.

However, as Web technologies have continued to advance rapidly, HTML has been pushed to its limits by developers and vendors. Ironically, the traits of HTML that helped build its popularity—its small size, limited number of elements, and ease of use—have become its downfall. HTML is a fixed specification with a finite set of elements. It's not **extensible**, meaning that you can't add new syntax or vocabulary to it. As a result of this limitation, Web developers and software vendors have stretched the usefulness of HTML almost to a breaking point. Browser vendors, such as Microsoft and Netscape, have added proprietary features and additional HTML elements to their browsers based on demands for more functionality, but in doing this they have compromised one of HTML's most important benefits—portability. Given these proprietary additions to particular browsers, HTML pages developed for use in one Web browser may not display in the same way when displayed in another browser or on another platform.

Despite all its benefits and the revolution it helped to spark, HTML has serious limitations that inhibit its future usefulness as Internet technologies continue to advance:

- HTML elements are used primarily for defining presentation and formatting styles, but they do not provide any information about the data itself.
- Because HTML has a limited number of elements, it lacks flexibility and extensibility and provides only a single, generic way to describe the data in a document.
- Searching the content of HTML documents produces poor results because of HTML's inability to recognize the function of data within a document.
- Until recently, Web browsers were the primary **client** program used to view content on the World Wide Web. With the introduction of new browsing technologies, such as wireless devices, voice and speech programs, personal digital assistants (PDAs), and so on, the limitations of HTML are increasingly troublesome.

An HTML Example

Let's look at an example that uses HTML and a Web browser. HTML provides a set of formatting and presentation **elements**—tags and content—that can be added to any text document. (You will see some tags in a moment.) Web browsers, such as Netscape Navigator and Internet Explorer, know how to interpret these HTML elements and present the document based on HTML's formatting rules.

> **TIP** To use an HTML element to format a piece of text, type the opening HTML **tag** (enclosed in brackets, as shown in the following example), then add the text to apply the format to, and then type the ending HTML tag. Here is an example:
>
> ```
> This text is bold
> ```
>
> The `<b>` and `</b>` HTML tags turn the formatting style "bold" on and off for the text "This text is bold." The entire piece of code, including the opening and ending tags along with the enclosed text, is known as an element. This piece of code would look like this in a Web browser:
>
> **This text is bold**

The following is a simple text document with no information added for formatting:

```
JOB POSTING
Job Title:  Web master

Job Description:  We are looking for a Web master to
oversee the management of our company's Web site.  The
Web master will be responsible for working with other
staff members to collect information for the Web site,
and for creating and maintaining the Web pages.

Skills needed:  Basic writing skills, good communication
skills, UNIX, HTML
```

Figure 1.3 shows what this plain text document looks like when viewed in Internet Explorer. As you can see, the Web browser can open the document, but without formatting instructions, it does not know how to correctly format it. HTML was designed to ignore all white-space characters, including line breaks, so without the proper HTML markup, this document displays as a block of text with no paragraph returns.

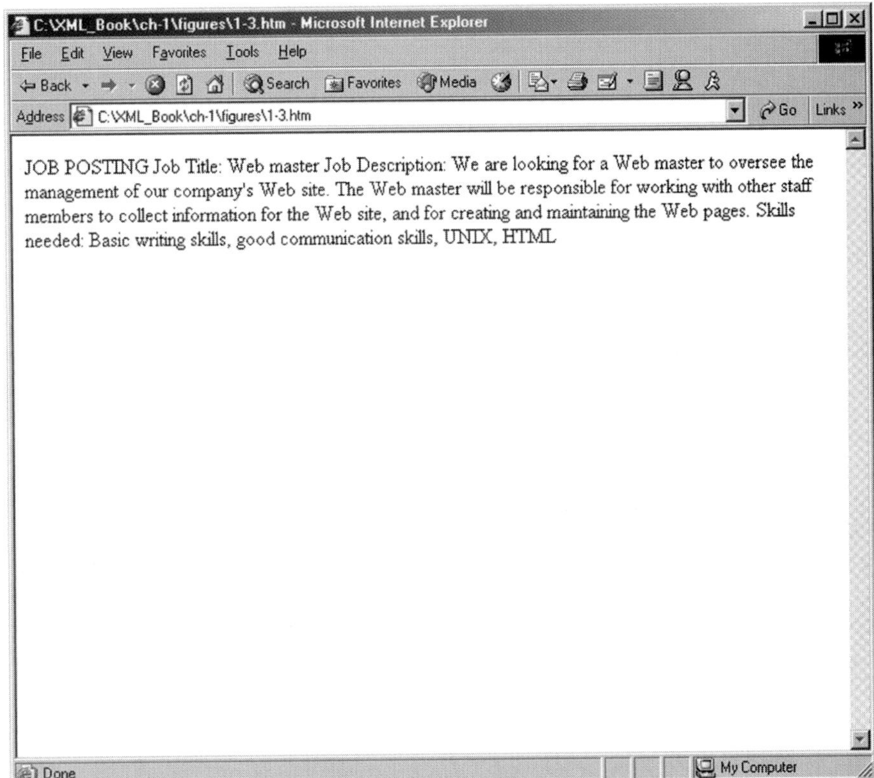

Figure 1.3 Unformatted Text Document Viewed in Internet Explorer

Now let's add some HTML elements to the document. Most HTML elements are used simply to turn certain formatting styles on and off. (Other elements provide additional functions, such as creating hyperlinks and displaying images, but this example uses only some of the basic formatting elements.) Here is the text document formatted as an HTML document:

```
1  <html>
2    <head>
3        <title>Job Posting: Web master</title>
4    </head>
5    <body>
6      <h1>JOB POSTING</h1>
7      <h2>Job Title:  <i>Web master</i></h2>
8      <p><b>Job Description:</b>
9      We are looking for a Web master to oversee the
10     management of our company's Web site.  The Web
11     master will be responsible for working with other
12     staff members to collect information for the Web
13     site, and for creating and maintaining the Web pages. </p>
14     <p><b>Skills needed:</b>  Basic writing skills, good
15     communication skills, HTML</p>
16   </body>
17 </html>
```

☆ **SHORTCUT** Follow these steps to do this example yourself:

1. Open a text editor on your computer, such as Notepad (on a Windows PC) or SimpleText (on a Macintosh).
2. Type the HTML code from the example, and save the document as `example1.html`. Do not include the line numbers.
3. Open your browser and click on the File menu.
4. Click on the Open or Open Page command, and choose the file `example1.html` that you saved.

The page will then be displayed in your browser.

This HTML document starts with an opening tag for the `html` element on line 1. Lines 2 through 4 describe the header section and the title of the document. The main body of the **document** begins on line 5 and ends on line 16. Lines 6 through 15 make up the body of the **page** and contain a mix of markup elements and content. The last line of the document, line 16, contains the closing tag for the `html` element. Notice that the beginning and ending tags for the `html` element—`<html>` and `</html>` on lines 1 and 17—enclose the entire document.

After adding HTML elements to the document, you can use a Web browser to open and display it with the formatting styles applied. As you can see in Figure 1.4, the document now contains formatting, as described by the HTML.

☆ **TIP** If you're not familiar with HTML, see "Online References" at the end of this chapter to find more information.

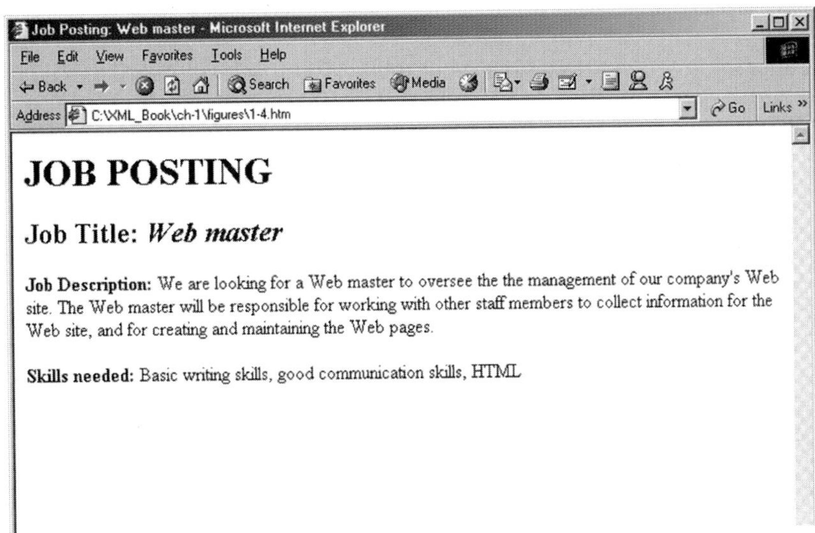

Figure 1.4 HTML Document Viewed in Internet Explorer

Enter XML: Why Is XML Needed?

The need for a new and better language became apparent as Web developers and vendors became more painfully aware of the limitations of HTML. In addition, the nature of the information displayed on the Internet began to change. The first generation of Web sites provided mostly static data that was easily stored as text, such as information about a company or product along with contact information. But then many companies began adding dynamic functions to their Web sites, such as transactions, which allow visitors to purchase items and services online. Web sites also started to rely heavily on data gathered from various sources, such as databases, news feeds, and other Web sites. Developers found themselves writing programs that would take data from various sources and then dynamically add HTML tags to format it as it was passed back to the Web browser to be displayed to viewers. This process was cumbersome and error-prone.

The W3C began work on XML in the mid-1990s, and the official XML version 1.0 specification was released in February 1998. The second edition of the 1.0 recommendation was released in October 2000. XML has quickly gained popularity in the Web community because it combines the simplicity of HTML with the flexibility and extensibility of SGML. In fact, XML is a subset of SGML. It is fully compatible with SGML and contains many of SGML's powerful features without much of the overhead, and that makes XML much more suited for developing programs to run on the Internet.

The Benefits of XML

As mentioned earlier, XML is not a markup language but rather is a set of tools that can be used to define and create new languages. Following are a few of the benefits of XML, many of which are discussed in this book:

- It allows the data to be self-describing, as opposed to being limited by a predefined set of elements.
- You can provide rules for XML elements that limit the type of data that an element can contain, such as only letters, only numbers, only certain values, or only a certain number of characters.
- It lets you create custom data structures for industry-specific or company-specific needs.
- Because XML describes data, the data can be displayed in any number of ways by applying different presentation styles.
- It provides a rich set of tools for linking.
- It can be used to interchange data between proprietary formats and between databases or data structures.
- The tools provided in XML can be used to define a standard syntax for many different markup languages.
- XML has robust and reliable data searching capabilities.

Separating Data from Presentation

One of the most important and powerful benefits of XML is that it separates the data, or content, of a document from the presentation and format. Unlike HTML elements, XML elements are designed to describe the data, not the format of the data. For example, the HTML tags `<p>` and `</p>` define the beginning and end of a paragraph, but these tags do not tell you anything about the content of the paragraph. It could contain a description of a product, directions to a restaurant, or a tutorial on how to program a VCR. These examples contain information about completely different things, but in HTML you would use the same `<p>` and `</p>` tags to define the beginning and end of the paragraph. In XML, on the other hand, you can create your own tags to describe the data. For example, you might use `<product-description>` and `</product-description>` as your beginning and ending tags, thereby describing the content of the data rather than its format.

Creating your own tags, however, creates more work for XML developers. The elements defined in XML documents are unique and do not inherently map to any particular formatting styles (as HTML elements do). This means that to create XML documents that have formatting such as bold or italic type, developers must create their own formatting styles using style sheets. A **style sheet** is a set of instructions that describes how to present the various elements in the XML document. Using the earlier `<product-description>` example, you would include instructions in the style sheet to tell a Web browser how to format this XML element. Perhaps you would define this element as a separate paragraph, putting two carriage returns before and after the paragraph. The style sheet could also instruct the browser to use a specific typeface, such as Arial, a specific point size, such as 12 points, and a color for the text, such as blue.

The benefit of the separation of content from presentation is that you can create multiple style sheets that will format the elements differently depending on how you want to use the data. For example, you could create one style sheet that contains formatting information for displaying your XML document in a Web browser, another style sheet for printing, and yet another style sheet for displaying the information on a wireless phone—each of which requires its own formatting instructions.

You can also use a single style sheet to provide formatting information for any number of XML documents. This comes in handy when you need to change a style in many documents. With HTML, to change a style on all your pages, you must modify each page or write a program that will modify the pages for you. If your Web site has a lot of pages, this becomes a daunting task. With XML, however, all you need to do is to change the style description in the style sheet. For example, you could change the color of the text for your `<product-description>` element from blue to orange, and that style would affect any XML document that uses your style sheet. Chapter Four explains in more detail how to create and use style sheets with XML documents.

Differences between XML and HTML

XML, like HTML, is an open standard and can be created and viewed using any text editor. Both HTML and XML are platform- and vendor-independent. Both XML and HTML use elements and tags to describe pieces of data within a document. However, XML is much more powerful and flexible than HTML. Following are some of the major differences between XML and HTML:

- XML is not dependent on a single document type or set of markup elements, as HTML is.
- Whereas the HTML specification defines a finite set of elements, XML allows you to define elements that best fit your document or data.
- XML separates presentation from data, thus overcoming one of the fundamental limitations of HTML.
- Web browsers are fairly "forgiving" in that they allow for poorly written HTML code to be displayed. If a browser encounters code that is written incorrectly, it can usually compensate and will display the content correctly. XML, on the other hand, is extremely strict about correct syntax.
- HTML tags are not case-sensitive. This means that an HTML page can contain an open tag written as `<blockquote>` and a closing tag written as `</BLOCKQUOTE>`, and the browser will interpret this as the opening and ending tags for a single element. XML, however, is case-sensitive, and an XML program would interpret these as two different element tags.

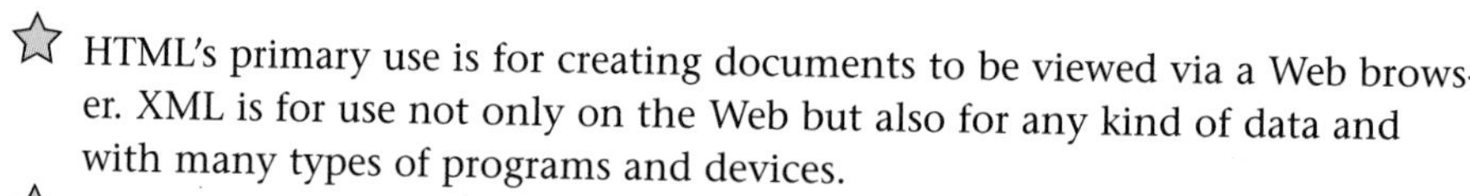

- HTML's primary use is for creating documents to be viewed via a Web browser. XML is for use not only on the Web but also for any kind of data and with many types of programs and devices.
- Because HTML's elements are built into Web browsers, it's easy to view a document with HTML formatting in the browser; all you need to do is to insert HTML tags into the document. Because XML's tags are user-defined, however, XML requires a little more work in order to present the data in a formatted fashion. The good news is that XML provides much more control over document style and layout.

At this point in its development, XML isn't meant to replace HTML on the Web. There are still millions of Web pages written in HTML that will remain as HTML documents for years to come. XML is simply meant as another, more flexible tool to use for Web development.

XHTML: The Best of Both Worlds

The current version of HTML, version 4.01, contains specifications on merging XML and HTML. W3C has proposed a new language that will merge the two technologies. Called XHTML, Extensible Hypertext Markup Language, this language uses HTML elements and XML's syntax rules.

XHTML allows for a quick transition to XML syntax for existing HTML documents by including the entire HTML 4.01 tag set in its specification. XHTML also allows authors to extend the current HTML tag set to define and include additional tags and combine XML vocabularies into one document. Because XML is much more strict about syntax rules, XHTML is a bit more challenging than HTML because it requires you to follow these rules and is not as forgiving of errors as Web browsers have traditionally been of HTML documents. For example, as mentioned earlier, HTML is not case-sensitive. XHTML, however, requires that all tags be written in lowercase. XHTML also requires that every element have a start tag and an end tag. HTML has many elements within its vocabulary that do not require end tags, such as the `<br>` and `<img>` tags. Some developers see this requirement to adhere to the rules as a positive step for HTML because it will force authors to write better code.

If you are interested in XHTML, pay close attention to the syntax rules covered in Chapter Two because they also apply to XHTML documents.

> ☆ **TIP** XHTML is already widely accepted by browsers: Netscape Navigator version 4 and later, and Internet Explorer 4 and later, recognize XHTML files.

Creating Your First XML Document

Now that you have a basic understanding of XML and some of its benefits, let's create a small XML document. Using the job description example from earlier in this chapter, here is how it might look as an XML document:

```
<?xml version="1.0"?>
<job-posting>
  <title>Job Title:  <emphasis>Web master</emphasis></title>
  <description>We are looking for a Web master to oversee
  the management of our company Web site.  The Web master
  will be responsible for working with other staff members
  to collect information for the Web site, and for creating
  and maintaining the Web pages.</description>
  <skill-list>
    <skill>Basic writing skills</skill>
    <skill>good communication skills</skill>
    <skill> XML</skill>
  </skill-list>
</job-posting>
```

☆ **SHORTCUT** To do this example yourself, follow the same steps as outlined for the HTML example from earlier in this chapter. However, to view the XML example in a browser, you need to use one that supports XML. Please see "Online References" at the end of the chapter for a link that provides information on which browser versions support XML.

This XML document looks a lot like the earlier HTML document except that this one uses different element names to describe the data. Remember that one of XML's strengths is that it separates data from presentation, so viewing this XML file in a Web browser won't produce a nice, formatted document as our HTML example did. The elements used in this example are unique and do not map to any particular formatting styles. To view this document with formatting, you would have to apply a style sheet. Figure 1.5 shows what this XML document looks like when viewed with Internet Explorer.

Notice the small + (plus) and – (minus) signs next to some of the lines in Figure 1.5. For example, the line `<skill-list>` has a small – next to it. XML documents create a tree-like structure, with leaves and branches. If you click on this minus sign, the skill list collapses, as in Figure 1.6. Now the minus sign has become a plus sign, which indicates that there is data contained within this element.

☆ **WARNING** Not all Web browsers have added XML support. You can refer to the "Browser XML Display Chart" Web page listed in "Online References" for current browser compatibility information. The examples in this book use Internet Explorer 6 and Netscape 6.

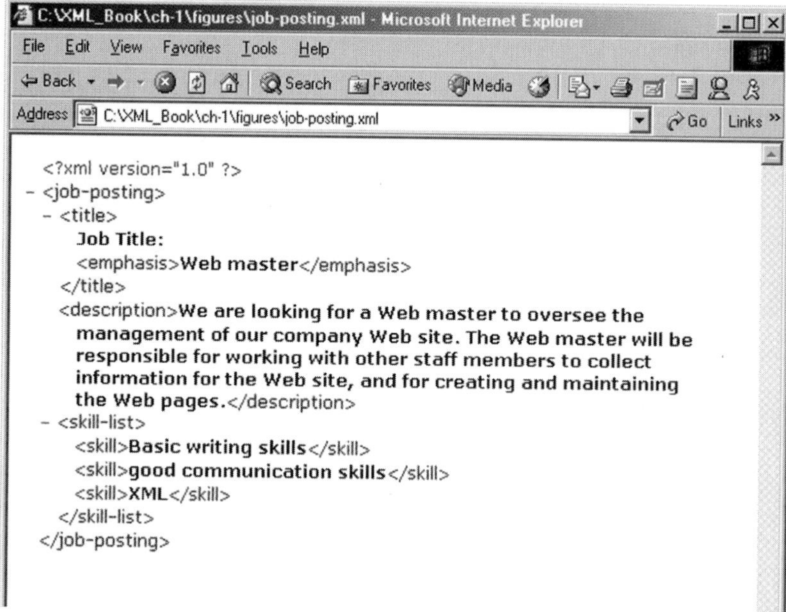

Figure 1.5 XML Document Viewed in Internet Explorer

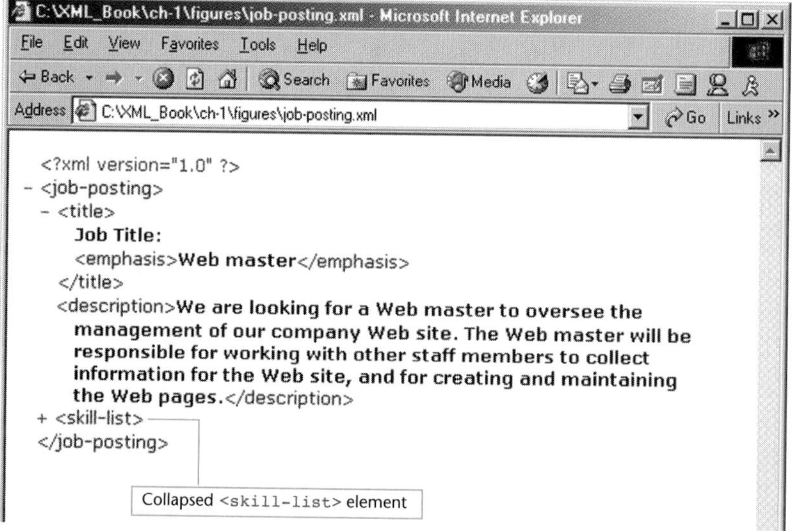

Figure 1.6 XML Document with the `<skill-list>` Element Collapsed

Looking closely at the XML file, you'll see that its syntax is similar to HTML. There are opening and closing tags, and elements in XML are defined in the same way they are defined in HTML: An element consists of an opening tag, a closing tag, and the content in between. In XML, the data has more of a hierarchy, however, and it is defined based on its function within the document and its relationship to other pieces of data. Elements that are contained within other elements are said to be **children**, and the elements that contain them are referred to as **parent** elements.

This idea of containing elements within other elements is called **nesting**. XML defines rules for elements and the nesting of tags within a document. Chapter Two describes these rules in more detail.

Figure 1.7 shows the element structure within our XML document, and Figure 1.8 shows the hierarchical relationships among the elements. In XML, each document contains a **root element**, which is an element that encompasses all the other elements in the document. In this case, `<job-posting>` is the root element.

```
<?xml version="1.0" ?>
<job-posting>
  <title>
    Job Title:
    <emphasis>Webmaster</emphasis>
  </title>
  <description>We are looking for a Webmaster to oversee the management of
    our company website. The Webmaster will be responsible for working with
    other staff members to collect information for the website, and for creating
    and maintaining the web pages.</description>
  <skill-list>
    <skill>Basic writing skills</skill>
    <skill>good communication skills</skill>
    <skill>HTML</skill>
  </skill-list>
</job-posting>
```

Figure 1.7 Element Structure in the Sample XML Document

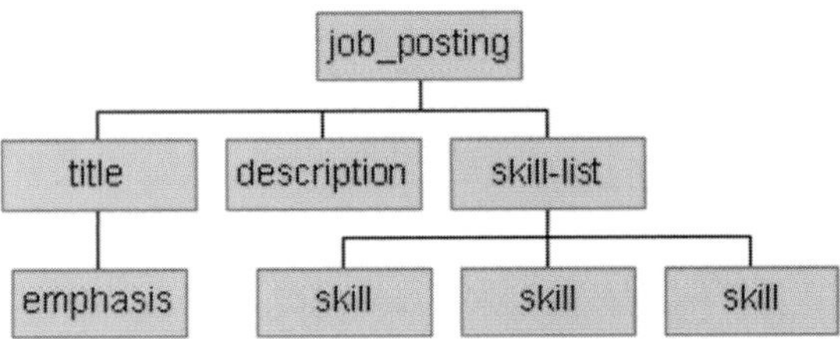

Figure 1.8 Relationships among Elements in the Sample XML Document

In this example, you have created your own set of tags to define the data for a job posting. Based on this XML document, you could use this data in many ways. You could use this XML document to present this job description on a Web page, print it in a report of open jobs, store the data in a database, or use it as input to a search program that would match it with certain search criteria. Notice how the XML document uses element names that describe the data, as opposed to the earlier HTML example, which used elements to define the presentation format only.

The following chapters describe in detail the various components that make up an XML document as well as other, complementary technologies being developed in conjunction with XML. Keep in mind that XML is still a fairly new technology and may change over the next few years. Therefore, keep a close eye on the XML specifications for changes. The W3C Web site (included in "Online References" at the end of this chapter) always has the latest draft of the XML specification. There, you'll find valuable information about other technologies being developed for XML, new uses for XML, and the direction XML is heading within the industry.

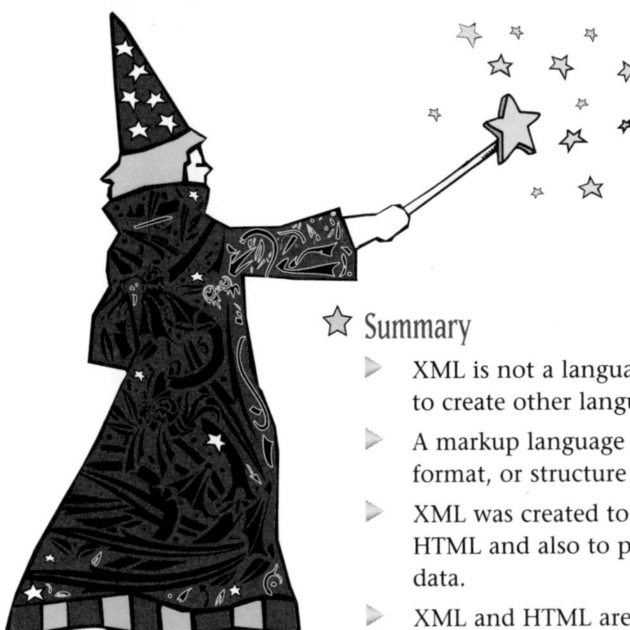

Summary

- XML is not a language, but a set of tools that can be used to create other languages.
- A markup language is a set of rules that defines the layout, format, or structure of the text within a document.
- XML was created to solve some of the problems with HTML and also to provide greater flexibility for defining data.
- XML and HTML are markup languages derived from SGML. They look somewhat alike but have important differences.
- XHTML combines HTML and XML, using HTML elements and XML's syntax rules.
- When you create an XML document, you use XML syntax rules to associate language elements with the content of your document. XML documents can be viewed using a Web browser.

Online References

The World Wide Web Consortium's XML Web site
`http://www.w3c.org/XML`

The XML Industry Portal
`http://www.xml.org/xml`

European Organization for Nuclear Research
`http://www.cern.ch/Public`

International Organization for Standardization
`http://www.iso.org`

HTML and XHTML home page (on the W3C Web site)
`http://www.w3.org/MarkUp`

Authoring HTML Basics
`http://hotwired.lycos.com/webmonkey/authoring/html_basics/index.html`

Microsoft's XML implementation, free tools, and browser information
`http://msdn.microsoft.com/xml`

Browser XML Display Chart
`http://www.xml.com/pub/a/2000/05/03/browserchart/`

☆Review Questions

1. What is a markup language?
2. Why is it important to have a cross-platform, vendor-independent file format such as HTML and XML?
3. What are some limitations of HTML?
4. What are some advantages of using XML over HTML?
5. What components make up an element?
6. Why is it a good idea to separate data from presentation?
7. List three differences between HTML and XML.
8. List two advantages that XHTML has over HTML.
9. What are some reasons for converting HTML documents to XHTML documents?

☆Hands-On Exercises

1. Go to the W3C Web site and locate the most recent XML recommendation.
2. Go to the W3C Web site and locate the most recent HTML and XHTML recommendations.
3. Create and save the HTML and XML documents for the "Job Posting" example in this chapter, and view them in a Web browser.
4. Create an XML document for the following:

   ```
   Camping Trip Gear List

   The following is a list of items that are essential
   on any camping trip:

   Flashlight
   Sleeping bag
   Lantern
   Bug Spray
   Compass
   ```
5. Open the document you created in Exercise 4 in a Web browser that supports XML, and click on the + (plus) and – (minus) signs to expand and collapse the elements. If your document creates an error message, try to determine the cause of the error.

A Closer Look at XML Documents

This chapter covers the various components, or building blocks, of XML along with the syntax rules for each of these components. Learning the rules for syntax and structure is essential to learning how to work with XML. By the end of this chapter, you should have a solid understanding of each of these components and know how to use them, how they are structured, and how they relate to one another.

Chapter Objectives

- To understand how the concept of syntax applies to XML
- To learn about the major components, or building blocks, that make up XML documents
- To learn the syntax rules for creating well-formed XML documents
- Learn how to use a parser to check the syntax of an XML document

XML Syntax

The term *syntax* refers to the rules of a language. As with any language, you must follow the syntax rules of XML in order for your document to make sense to the program that processes the information. Let's use the English language for comparison. English has rules about how to form sentences so that the information is presented in a conventional manner that readers or listeners can understand. If people were to speak or write English in a way that did not follow the basic syntax of the language, you would have a hard time understanding the meaning they were trying to convey.

For example, one English syntax rule says that every sentence must have a noun and a verb, typically in that order. Without both of these word types, the sentence is not complete. Here is an example of a simple, but grammatically complete, sentence: "The dog ran." This sentence isn't very exciting, but it is complete and creates a valid English sentence with a noun followed by a verb. Sentences that don't follow this basic rule don't make sense—for example, "The dog" or "ran The dog."

English also has rules about adding information beyond the basic noun-verb structure. You can, for example, add an adjective and an adverb to make the sentence more descriptive: "The fat dog ran slowly." Here, *fat* is an adjective that describes the dog; in English (although not in some other languages), the adjective usually precedes the noun it modifies. *Slowly* is an adverb that describes how the dog ran; in English, the adverb is usually placed as close as possible to the verb it modifies. Again, breaking the rules would result in a sentence that doesn't make sense: "fat slowly dog ran The."

Like English, XML has a set of language rules that you, as an XML author, must follow. Let's look at the various components that make up the language. Then we will cover the syntax rules along with ways you can check the syntax of your XML documents.

Components of XML Documents

Like an English sentence, each XML document has a number of required and optional components. This section takes a close look at the pieces that make up an XML document.

The XML Declaration

The XML **declaration** tells the program that is reading the document that it is an XML document, along with other optional information. The declaration always appears as the first line in an XML document. It cannot be preceded by any blank lines or white space. The declaration tag begins with `<?xml` and ends with `?>`. The XML declaration can contain the following three attributes: `version`, `encoding`, and `standalone`. (Attributes are discussed later in this chapter.) Although the XML declaration is optional in XML, it is good practice to at least declare the version of XML being used:

```
<?xml version="1.0"?>
```

Currently, the only released version of XML is 1.0, but this will change in the future. Declaring the version that your document is using will help parsers (discussed later in this chapter) and other programs interpret the document if future versions of XML differ from the current 1.0 specification.

The second piece of information that the declaration can contain is the `encoding` attribute, which defines the **character set** that the document uses. A character set is a grouping of characters. Some examples are the Latin character set (such as a, b, c, A, B, C), a character set of symbols (such as +, §, and _), or a character set of Greek letters (such as α, β, and Ω). The `encoding` attribute is optional in the XML declaration; if no character set is defined, the default character set is UTF-8, which is the 8-bit Unicode character-encoding scheme. Other character sets are UTF-16, UTF-32, and ISO-10646-UCS-2.

```
<?xml version="1.0" encoding="UTF-8"?>
```

☆**TIP** All XML processors (programs that know how to work with XML files) are required to handle UTF-8, and that is why it is the default character set. Most of them can also handle UTF-16. There are hundreds of character sets you can use in your documents, but they aren't covered in this book. For more information about character sets, see "Online References" at the end of the chapter.

The third piece of information that the XML declaration can contain is the `standalone` attribute. The value of this attribute must be either "`yes`" or "`no`." This attribute is also optional, and the default value is "`no`". This attribute tells the processor whether this document contains all the pertinent information within itself or instead relies on external **document type definitions** (DTDs) for its declarations (DTDs are covered in Chapter Three). Setting this value to "`yes`" tells the processor that everything needed to process the document is within the document and tells it to ignore any references to external files. Setting the value to "`no`" tells the processor that the document can reference external files.

```
<?xml version="1.0" encoding="UTF-8" standalone="no"?>
```

XML Elements

Elements, the core component of XML documents, are used to describe the data in a document. An element consists of three pieces:

- A **start tag**: the name of the element surrounded by the < and > characters (`<element>`)
- **Content**: data or other elements or both
- An **end tag**: a forward slash and the name of the element surrounded by the < and > characters (`</element>`)

XML elements are like English nouns: They are definable objects that can contain other pieces of information such as elements, attributes, content, and so on. Here are some examples of elements:

```
<book>Content</book>
<email_message>Content</email_message>
<transaction>Content</transaction>
<bank_account>Content</bank_account>
<project>Content</project>
```

☆ **WARNING** Even though XML allows you to create your own element names, there are rules about creating names. You will learn these rules later in this chapter when we discuss well-formed documents.

Figure 2.1 shows an example of an element with the pieces labeled.

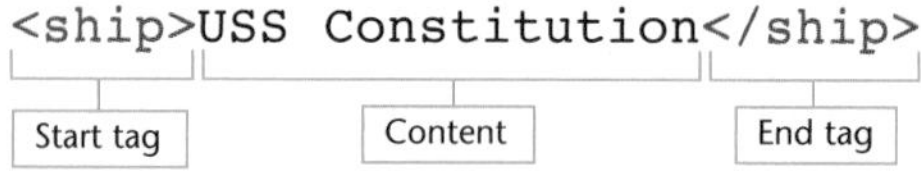

Figure 2.1 An XML Element

The Root Element

All XML documents contain an outermost element called the **root element**. This element defines the type of object the XML document represents. All other elements and data within the document further describe the root element. For example, if you wanted to describe a book, you would create a document with a `<book>` root element. The other elements in the document would further describe the book, such as `<title>`, `<author>`, `<publisher>`, `<publish_date>`, and so on.

Child Elements and Nesting

Elements can act as **containers** for other pieces of information, including other elements and content. In our "book" example, the `<book>` element is the container for the other elements that describe the book.

Let's cover some terminology:

- **Nesting** refers to the process of containing elements within other elements.
- **Child** elements are elements that are contained within other elements.
- **Parent** elements are elements that contain other elements.
- **Sibling** elements are elements that share the same parent element.

You can make the hierarchy of element nesting as deep as you need to, depending on the complexity of the data you are describing. XML has no limit on nesting depth.

Let's look at another example, this one using a family tree. The parents—Sally and Joe—have three children: Larry, Curly, and Mo:

```
<family_tree>
    <mother>Sally</mother>
    <father>Joe</father>
    <children>
        <child>Larry</child>
        <child>Curly</child>
        <child>Mo</child>
    </children>
</family_tree>
```

The root element

Siblings

Parent element of the three <child> elements

In this example, the root element is <family_tree>. Within its start and end tags, the root element has the following three child elements : <mother>, <father>, and <children>. The element <children> also has child elements: the three <child> elements. In this example, the three <child> elements are all siblings because they share a common parent element, <children>.

Empty Elements

Empty elements are used primarily to describe pieces of data that don't have any content. Some common empty elements in HTML are
 (line break), <img> (image), and <p> (paragraph). XML provides a simple syntax to represent empty elements. They are only single tag elements, meaning that they have a start tag, but do not require an ending tag. Here is an example of an empty element:

```
<picture/>
```

Empty elements, unlike other elements, have only one tag. The syntax is similar to a start tag but includes a forward slash (/) before the ending > character. Empty elements follow the same rules as other XML elements. The three HTML elements in the preceding paragraph would be written as follows in XML:
 (line break), <img/> (image), and <p/> (paragraph).

XML Attributes

Now that you understand the concepts of XML elements, let's take a look at attributes, the second building block component. **Attributes** are pieces of information that help to describe or label XML elements. In the sentence you looked at earlier in the chapter—"The fat dog ran slowly"—the adjective *fat* is used to describe the noun *dog*. It does not change the meaning of *dog*; it simply adds more detail about the dog. An XML attribute works in the same way. Let's first look at the syntax of an attribute and then look at how attributes are used.

> ☆**TIP** An element can have any number of attributes. However, having too many attributes can be confusing. If you find yourself using more than a few attributes for a given element, you may want to consider using additional elements for some of the data.

Attributes are always contained within the start tag of an element, are case-sensitive, and must have a value. Attributes are referred to as **name-value pairs** and have the following syntax: The name of the attribute is on the left, followed by an equal sign, and then the value. The value of an attribute must be surrounded by either single or double quotes. Here are a few examples:

```
<property address="123 Main Street" city="Boston" state="MA">
...</property>
<movie source="http://www.movies.com/files/movie.mpg">...</movie>
<composer name='Bach'>...</composer>
```

Attributes

The attributes defined for each of the elements describe something about the element. The attributes for `<property>` (`address`, `city`, and `state`) and `<composer>` (`name`) provide more details about the element, and the attribute for `<movie>` defines the location of the file on the Internet. Empty XML elements can also contain attributes. If the `<movie>` (`source`) element in the preceding example were an empty element, it would be written this way:

```
<movie source="http://www.movies.com/files/movie.mpg"/>
```

For a given piece of information, should you use elements or attributes? The answer to that question is subjective. It is up to the author and is based on the nature of the data. The following examples provide the same information as the examples shown earlier, but here we use elements instead of attributes:

```
<property>
  <address>123 Main Street</address>
  <city>Boston</city>
  <state>MA</state>
</property>
```

```
<movie>
  <source>http://www.movies.com/files/movie.mpg</source>
</movie>
```

```
<composer>
  <name>Bach</name>
</composer>
```

When you're trying to decide whether to use elements or attributes, ask yourself these questions:

- Does the piece of data contain child elements? If it does, use an element because attributes cannot have child elements.
- Does the piece of data contain a large amount of text? Although the value of an attribute can be large, it is good programming practice to contain large blocks of content within an element.

XML Entities

Entities, the third major XML building block, are one of the features that make XML so powerful. **Entities** are used as placeholders for content in an XML document. They can contain many different types of data, including text, special characters, XML markup, and binary data. XML has two types of entities: general and parameter. This chapter covers only general entities.

General entities are placeholders for any information that is contained within the root element of an XML document. General entities fall into three types:

- **Character** entities: used in place of special characters
- **Content** entities: used to mark the place of a common block of content that you type often or that may change
- **Unparsed** entities: used for binary or other nontext data, such as an image or video clip

Character Entities

Certain characters, such as the tag delimiter characters (< and >), have special meaning in XML. It is illegal in XML to use these characters in the content of an element because a program that is processing the XML document will interpret them as part of the tag syntax, and that will result in an error. Here is a small XML document that causes an error:

```
1    <?xml version="1.0"?>
2    <equation>  50 < 100 </equation>
```

Error in syntax

☆ **SHORTCUT** Here's how to see the error message. Type the two lines of code into your favorite text editor (do not type the line numbers at the beginning of the lines), save the code onto your hard drive, and open it with Internet Explorer (version 5.0 or later).

This document will create an error message if you open it in Internet Explorer. Figure 2.2 shows the error message that is displayed. Internet Explorer's built-in XML parser thinks that the less-than sign between 50 and 100 should be part of the markup.

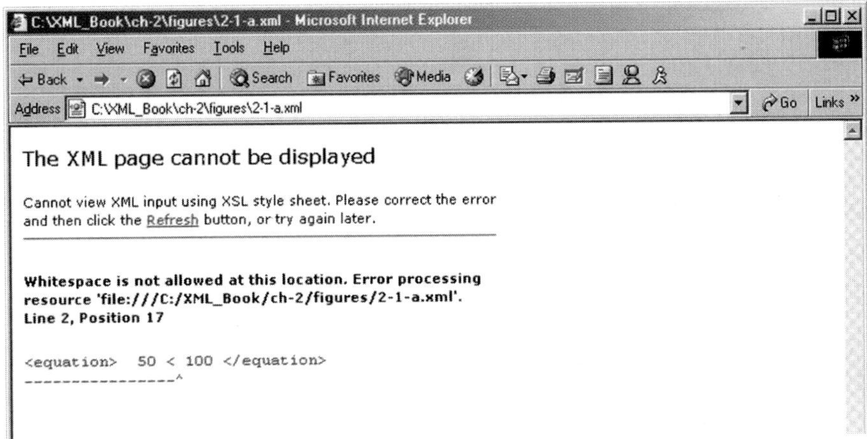

Figure 2.2 Error Produced by Internet Explorer

To solve this problem, you must replace the less-than sign (<) with its character entity reference: `<`. The syntax for a character entity is an ampersand (`&`) followed by the entity name, or code (here, `lt`), and ending with a semicolon (`;`).

There are two types of character entities: named and numbered. XML supports the Unicode character set, which consists of hundreds of numbers, letters, and symbols. Common symbols are given **entity names** so that they are easier to remember. For other characters, you can use the corresponding Unicode decimal or hexadecimal number to represent the entity. The "Online References" section later in the chapter tells you where you can find more information about character sets and their corresponding reference numbers. Table 2.1 lists some named character entities.

Table 2.1 Names and Decimal Values for a Few Character Entities

Character	Name	Decimal	Entity References
'	apos	39	' or '
"	quot	34	" or "
>	gt	62	> or >
<	lt	60	< or <

To use a character entity in a document, type the entity reference in place of the character you wish to display. Let's fix the example from earlier in this section:

```
<?xml version="1.0"?>
<equation>  50 &lt; 100 </equation>
```

Character entity

☆ SHORTCUT Type the two lines into your favorite text editor (do not type the line numbers at the beginning of the lines), save it onto your hard drive, and open it with Internet Explorer (version 5.0 or later). You will see that the error message is now gone.

Figure 2.3 shows a much happier XML parser. Notice that the Internet Explorer parser replaced the character entity with the less than symbol (<).

Content Entities

The second type of general entity is a content entity. You can define these entities yourself and use them to replace content anywhere in your XML document. This powerful XML feature allows you to change a piece of content in one place and have those changes take effect everywhere the entity is referenced. If you are familiar with programming languages, these types of entities are like variables.

You can use content entities to create **boilerplate** documents: standardized documents that can be customized by changing the value of entity references. You'll see an example in a moment. Content entities can contain any kind of valid content, including XML markup.

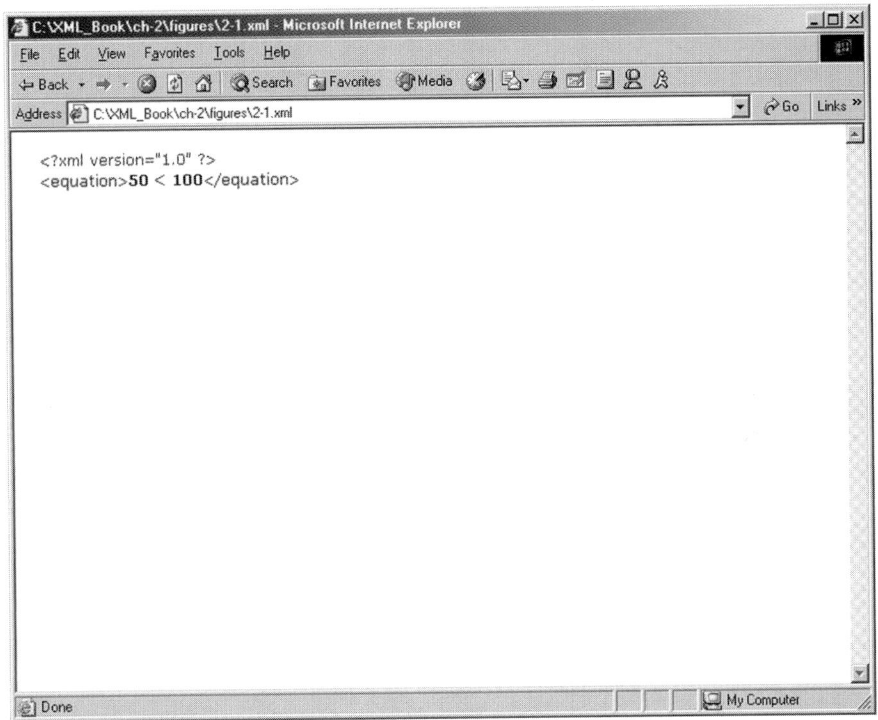

Figure 2.3 Character Entity Example

Content entities are defined within the **internal subset** of a DTD, which is the part of the DTD defined within the XML document. Chapter Three covers the details of DTDs and the `DOCTYPE` declaration, so don't worry if this syntax looks a little confusing.

Entities are defined within a document after the XML declaration and before the start of the root element. The content of an entity can be declared inside the XML file, or it can reside in a separate file. Entity declarations that are defined inside the XML file are called **internal entities**, and ones that reside in separate files are **external entities**. Let's look first at internal entities. Following is an example of an internal entity declaration that replaces the entity `&address;` with a street address:

```
<!ENTITY address "123 Main Street">
```

The syntax for an internal entity declaration consists of `<!ENTITY` followed by the reference name—in this case, `address`—and then the text string for the address, enclosed in quotes. As with attributes, you can use either single or double quotes, as long as you are consistent. To use this entity in a document, place its reference notation (`&address;`) at the place or places within your document where you want the address to appear. You can place it as many times as you like throughout your document.

Here is an example of an XML document, with internal entity declarations for company information: name, address, city, state, and zip. Figure 2.4 shows what the parsed document looks like in Internet Explorer.

```
<?xml version="1.0"?>
<!DOCTYPE business [
<!ENTITY name "ACME Shipping Company">
<!ENTITY address "123 Main Street">
<!ENTITY city "Boston">
<!ENTITY state "MA">
<!ENTITY zip "02109">
]>
<business>
   <business_name>Business Name: &name;</business_name>
   <business_address>Business Address: &address;
   </business_address>
   <business_city>Business City: &city;</business_city>
   <business_state>Business State: &state;</business_state>
   <business_zip>Business Zip Code: &zip;</business_zip>
   <shipping_address>Shipping Address: &address;
   </shipping_address>
   <shipping_city>Shipping City: &city;</shipping_city>
   <shipping_state>Shipping State: &state;</shipping_state>
   <shipping_zip>Shipping Zip Code: &zip;</shipping_zip>
</business>
```

Entity references in XML content

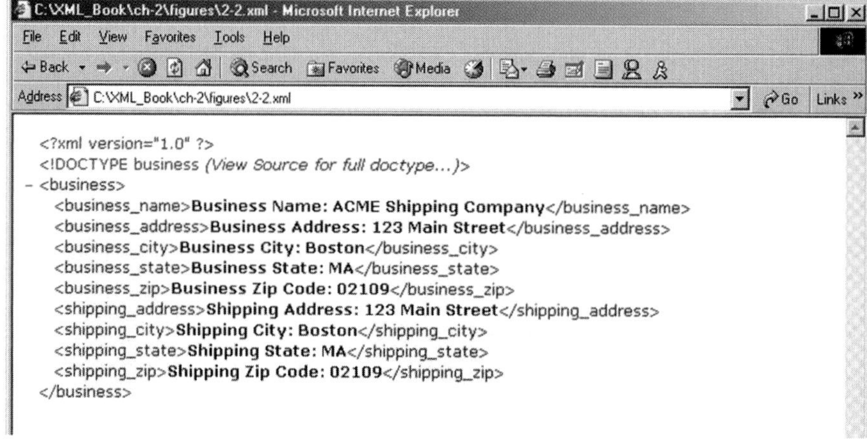

C:\XML_Book\ch-2\figures\2-2.xml - Microsoft Internet Explorer
File Edit View Favorites Tools Help
Back Search Favorites Media
Address C:\XML_Book\ch-2\figures\2-2.xml
Go Links
<?xml version="1.0" ?>
<!DOCTYPE business (View Source for full doctype...)>
- <business>
<business_name>Business Name: ACME Shipping Company</business_name>
<business_address>Business Address: 123 Main Street</business_address>
<business_city>Business City: Boston</business_city>
<business_state>Business State: MA</business_state>
<business_zip>Business Zip Code: 02109</business_zip>
<shipping_address>Shipping Address: 123 Main Street</shipping_address>
<shipping_city>Shipping City: Boston</shipping_city>
<shipping_state>Shipping State: MA</shipping_state>
<shipping_zip>Shipping Zip Code: 02109</shipping_zip>
</business>

Figure 2.4 Parsed XML Document with Entity Declarations

Each entity for the address information—address, city, state, and zip—is referenced twice within the XML document in lines 9 through 19 to help demonstrate how entities work. If you change any of the information in the declarations (lines 3 through 7), it will automatically change the content everywhere this reference exists in the document. Let's say the company in this example moves to a different street address: 15 Another Street. Here is the XML document again with a new street address in the declaration. Figure 2.5 shows what it looks like in Internet Explorer.

```
1  <?xml version="1.0"?>
2  <!DOCTYPE business [
3  <!ENTITY name "ACME Shipping Company">
4  <!ENTITY address "15 Another Street">
5  <!ENTITY city "Boston">
6  <!ENTITY state "MA">
7  <!ENTITY zip "02109">
8  ]>
9  <business>
10    <business_name>Business Name: &name;</business_name>
11    <business_address>Business Address: &address;
      </business_address>
12    <business_city>Business City: &city;</business_city>
13    <business_state>Business State: &state;</business_state>
14    <business_zip>Business Zip Code: &zip;</business_zip>
15    <shipping_address>Shipping Address: &address;
      </shipping_address>
16    <shipping_city>Shipping City: &city;</shipping_city>
17    <shipping_state>Shipping State: &state;</shipping_state>
18    <shipping_zip>Shipping Zip Code: &zip;</shipping_zip>
19 </business>
```

Modified entity value

The new value will be inserted everywhere the entity is referenced.

Without using an entity for the address, you would have to go through the entire document and make all the address changes manually. This task could be time-consuming and error-prone if the document is large and contains many occurrences of the company's address. However, if you use an entity declaration for the address and use the entity reference everywhere in the document where you want the address to appear, you simply change the declaration to the new address. All the references will automatically be updated when the document is parsed.

Now let's look at external entities. In our example, suppose a description of the company is located in a separate file called `description.xml`. Figure 2.6 shows the content of this file.

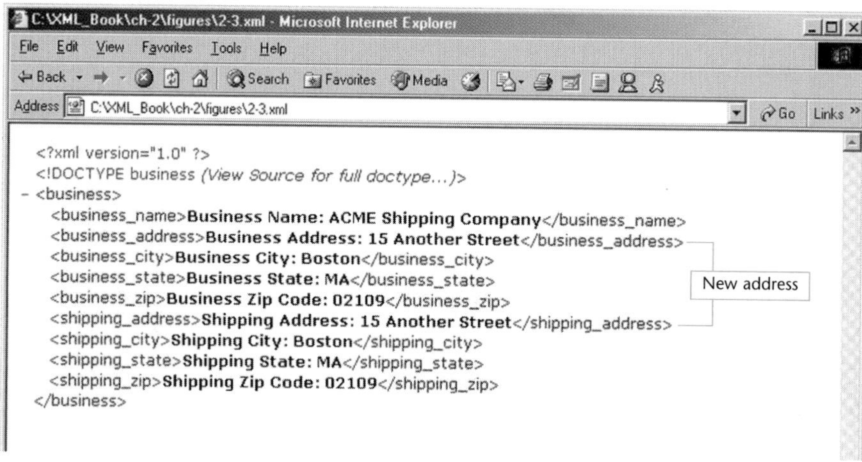

Figure 2.5 Parsed XML Document with Modified `address` Entity

```
<business_description>Description:  The ACME Shipping
company guarantees same-day shipping anywhere in the
world!</business_description>
```

Figure 2.6 The `description.xml` File

☆ **SHORTCUT** Use an external entity declaration for information that will be used in multiple XML documents. If you need to change the information, all you have to do is update the file, and each file that references it will automatically be updated with the new information.

Here is the entity declaration statement to refer to this file as the content of the entity:

```
<!ENTITY description SYSTEM "description.xml">
```

The syntax for an external entity declaration consists of `<!ENTITY` followed by the reference name—in this case, `description`—then the keyword **`SYSTEM`** (to indicate that the content resides outside the current XML document), and then the location of the file, enclosed in quotes. This file happens to reside in the same directory as our original file, but you can reference a document anywhere on the Internet by using the full Internet address to locate the file.

☆ **TIP** If the file description.xml were located on a server on the Internet called `www.acme.com`, the declaration would look like this:

```
<!ENTITY description SYSTEM "http://www.acme.com/description.xml">
```

Here is the document again with the external entity declaration added:

```
<?xml version="1.0"?>
<!DOCTYPE business [
<!ENTITY name "ACME Shipping Company">
<!ENTITY address "15 Another Street">
<!ENTITY city "Boston">
<!ENTITY state "MA">
<!ENTITY zip "02109">
<!ENTITY description SYSTEM "description.xml">
]>
<business>
   <business_name>Business Name: &name;</business_name>
   <business_address>Business Address: &address;
   </business_address>
   <business_city>Business City: &city;</business_city>
   <business_state>Business State: &state;</business_state>
   <business_zip>Business Zip Code: &zip;</business_zip>
   <shipping_address>Shipping Address: &address;
   </shipping_address>
   <shipping_city>Shipping City: &city;</shipping_city>
   <shipping_state>Shipping State: &state;</shipping_state>
   <shipping_zip>Shipping Zip Code: &zip;</shipping_zip>
   &description;
</business>
```

This is an external entity reference to a file called description.xml.

The data in this file will be inserted everywhere the entity is referenced.

Figure 2.7 shows the new document after it has been parsed in Internet Explorer.

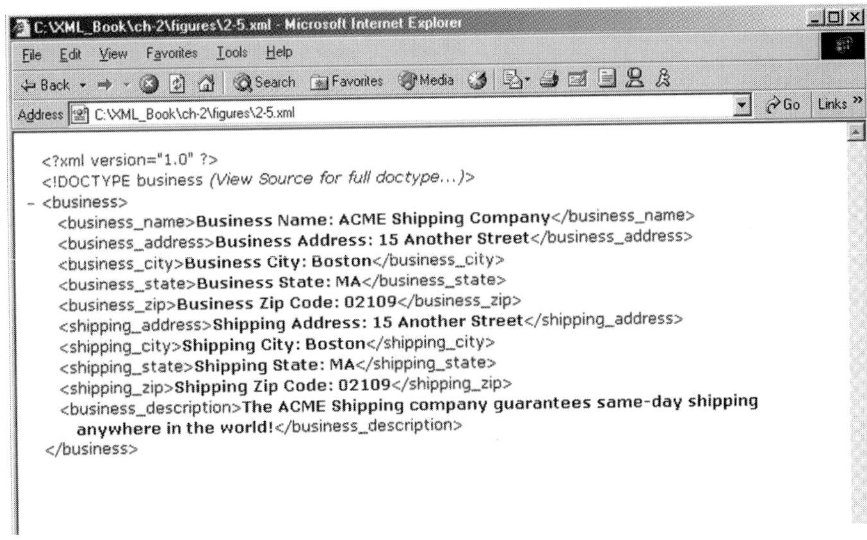

Figure 2.7 Parsed XML Document with External Entity Declaration

Unparsed Entities

Some types of data contain information other than text. This data, such as image or video files, should not be parsed like other XML data. An **unparsed entity** declaration tells the processing program not to parse the data but instead to pass it through as-is. Here is an example:

```
<!ENTITY picture SYSTEM "sunset.gif" NDATA GIF>
```

The syntax is similar to an external entity declaration, with a few additional pieces of information at the end. The keyword **NDATA** stands for "notation data," and the keyword **GIF** refers to the type of file this entity refers to, in this case a graphics file. Of course, the program that processes the XML document must know how to display or otherwise process files of this type in order to do anything useful with them.

XML Comments

Comments in XML are notes that are ignored by parsers. You can use comments to document your code, add information about a piece of data, insert visual breaks, or add information that other people working on or using your document would find useful. Following is an example of a comment:

```
<!-- This is a comment -->
```

The syntax of XML comments is the same as that of comments in HTML. They start with `<!--`, followed by the content of the comment, followed by `-->`. Following are more examples:

```
<!-- New element begins here -->
<!-- The purpose of the document is to provide a
structure for defining job postings -->
<!-- ################################################ -->
<!-- Changes made by Cheryl on May 28, 2000 -->
```

Well-Formed XML Documents

Now that you are familiar with the major building blocks of XML, let's look at the rules for using them. An XML document that adheres to XML syntax rules is said to be **well formed**. A document that is not well formed will generate an error in a parser program.

XML has few rules, and they are fairly easy to learn. Following are the syntax rules for writing well-formed XML documents:

- All XML documents must contain one (and only one) root element.
- All elements must have a start and an end tag—for example: `<article>...</article>`. The exception is an empty element, which must have a / before the end tag: `<image/>` is the same as writing `<image></image>`. This element does not have any content between the tags and can be written either way as valid XML.

Elements must be nested properly and cannot overlap. Each element must be contained completely inside its parent element. This rule is the same as for math functions. Here is a sample math equation:

```
(A * [B + C] )
```

Notice that this equation has two parts: one that is surrounded by the (and) characters, and a second one that is surrounded by [and]. The subequation [B + C] is entirely contained within the outer equation, which is delineated by the (and) characters. It is illegal to write the equation this way:

```
(A * [B + C ) ]
```

Here, the outer equation is ended,), before the inner one,].

This same rule applies to nesting elements in XML. Here is an example of illegal element nesting:

```
<book><chapter>...</book></chapter>
```

In this example, the ending tags for <book> and <chapter> overlap. This is illegal in XML and will cause a parsing error.

Here is an example of legal nesting of elements:

```
<book><chapter>...</chapter></book>
```

Here, the chapter element is correctly closed before the book element.

All attributes must have a value, and it must be enclosed in quotes. Double or single quotes are allowed and can be nested, but you must be consistent and use the same type of quote for the value. Here are some valid examples:

```
<salutation value='Hello'>
<salutation value="Hello">
```

In the following example of using nested quotes, double quotes surround the entire value of the attribute, and single quotes are used to quote the string "Hello" within the value:

```
<salutation value="We say 'Hello' to greet someone">
```

TIP A string is simply a group of character data, like a word or a sentence. It can also be a group of numbers and letters that represent something, like a part number or an acronym. Here are a few examples of string values:

Horse
The horse was in the barn
45 Summer Ave.
IRS
COMP123

Attributes must be placed in the start tag of an element, and no attribute can appear more than once. Here is an example of an illegal attribute listing:

```
<fleet ship_name="Nina" ship_name="Pinta"
ship_name="Santa Maria"></fleet>
```

It is illegal to have attributes with the same name within one element.

In the preceding example, the attribute name `ship_name` appears three times, and that is illegal in XML syntax. You can change the names of the attributes to make this legal:

```
<fleet ship_name1="Nina" ship_name2="Pinta"
ship_name3="Santa Maria"></fleet>
```

Now it is legal—the attributes have different names.

In this example, each attribute now has a unique name: `ship_name1`, `ship_name2`, and `ship_name3`.

Element names are case-sensitive. For example, `<TITLE>` and `</title>` are considered two separate elements in XML and would cause an error if both did not have a start and an end tag.

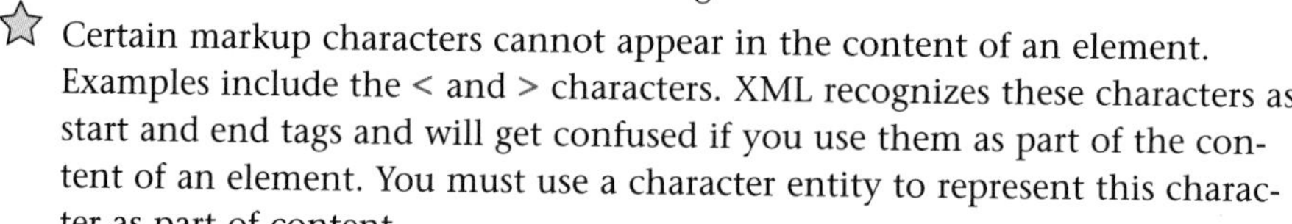

Certain markup characters cannot appear in the content of an element. Examples include the < and > characters. XML recognizes these characters as start and end tags and will get confused if you use them as part of the content of an element. You must use a character entity to represent this character as part of content.

Element names can start with letters or an underscore and can contain only letters, numbers, hyphens, periods, and underscores. They cannot start with `xml`, and they cannot contain spaces. Here are examples of legal element names:

```
<first_name>
<_first.name>
<first-name>
```

The following are illegal element names:

`<first name>` (illegal space)
`<first*name>` (illegal "*" character)
`<2-firstname>` (cannot start with a number)
`<xml_firstname>` (cannot start with "`xml`")

☆**WARNING** If you are familiar with HTML you will notice many similarities to XML syntax, but notice that XML is much more strict than HTML. HTML browsers, such as Internet Explorer and Netscape Navigator, are very forgiving of poorly written HTML code, and an HTML document that has errors will usually display OK in a browser window. Even a small error in XML, on the other hand, will produce an error in a parser. Knowing HTML will help you make the transition to XML, but you must be careful to follow the XML rules to avoid errors in your documents.

XML Parsers

An XML **parser** is a program that checks your XML document to ensure that you have followed the rules and that your document is well formed. There are two kinds of parsers: validating and nonvalidating. A **nonvalidating** parser reads your XML document and looks for syntax errors according to the language rules. A **validating** XML parser checks your document against a DTD or schema (covered in Chapter Three). If your document contains errors, the parser will display an error message and may even tell you the location of the error.

Parsers work like **compilers**, especially C++ or Java compilers, checking the document to make sure that it conforms to the grammatical structure of the language specification and that you have not omitted anything such as an end tag or a quote. It is a good idea to fix parser errors from the top down. Often, an error at the top of a document causes more errors later in the document, so fixing this error may eliminate others.

☆**TIP** The latest versions of Internet Explorer and Netscape Navigator contain XML parsers. See the appendix on XML tools for more information about parsers.

Summary

- XML is flexible, but it has a few syntax language rules that must be followed.
- The major components of XML are elements, attributes, entities, and comments.
- Elements define the pieces of data in an XML document. They are like nouns in a sentence.
- Attributes are used to further describe elements. They are like adjectives and adverbs in a sentence.
- There are three types of general entities: character, content, and unparsed entities.
- Comments can be used to provide information within the document and are not parsed.
- Documents that conform to the rules of XML are called well-formed documents.
- A parser is a software program that checks the syntax of an XML document.

Online References

W3C XML 1.0 Specification (Second Edition)
`http://www.w3.org/TR/REC-xml`

Section of XML 1.0 specification devoted to well-formed XML documents
`http://www.w3.org/TR/REC-xml#sec-well-formed`

W3C - International Character Set
`http://www.w3.org/International/O-charset.html`

Unicode Web site
`http://www.unicode.org`

IANA (Internet Assigned Numbers Authority)
`http://www.iana.org`

Review Questions

1. Explain why it's important to adhere to the syntax rules for XML.
2. Why is it important to declare the version of XML that a document is using?
3. Explain the concept of element nesting.
4. What is the relationship between a parent and a child element?
5. What are attributes, and where in the element syntax are they defined?

6. Why can't the less-than character (<) be used in XML content? What type of entity would you use to reference this character?
7. Explain the difference between internal and external content entities.
8. What is a well-formed XML document, and what type of program can be used to check whether a document is well formed?

☆Hands-On Exercises

1. Find the five syntax errors in the following XML code:

```
<?xml version="1.0"?>
<shopping_list>
  <item on_sale="yes>Milk</item>
  <item on_sale="no">Apples<item>
  <item on_sale="yes">Paper towels
  <Item on_sale="no">Soda</item>
</shopping list>
```

2. Create well-formed XML documents for the following two examples:

   a.
```
Student Grades for "Introduction to XML" course
Jane Smith:  B
Tony Adams:  C
John Myers:  B
Sandy Evans:  A
```

   b.
```
Project Information
Purpose of Project:
  "The purpose of this project is to create an
  internal staffing department so that the company
  is not dependent on external firms to recruit new
  employees"
Project Manager:  Anita Salyer
Project ID:  HR1234
Project Meeting Time:  Wednesday, 3:00 PM
Target Completion Date:  August 9
```

3. Create internal content entities for the content in the following XML elements, and replace the content with the entity references: <to>, <from>, and <subject>.

```
<?xml version="1.0"?>
<memo>
   <to>John Jones</to>
   <from>C Hughes</from>
   <subject>Time to learn more about XML</subject>
</memo>
```

4. Use an XML parser, such as Internet Explorer version 5.0 or later, to check your work on Exercises 1 through 4 to verify that your documents are well formed.

5. Create the XML document with entity references from earlier in the chapter, and complete steps a through e that follow. Name the file `business.xml`. Following is the document:

```
<?xml version="1.0"?>
<!DOCTYPE business [
<!ENTITY name "ACME Shipping Company">
<!ENTITY address "15 Another Street">
<!ENTITY city "Boston">
<!ENTITY state "MA">
<!ENTITY zip "02109">
<!ENTITY description SYSTEM "description.xml">
]>
<business>
  <business_name>Business Name: &name;</business_name>
  <business_address>Business Address: &address;
  </business_address>
  <business_city>Business City: &city;</business_city>
  <business_state>Business State: &state;
  </business_state>
  <business_zip>Business Zip Code: &zip;
  </business_zip>
  <shipping_address>Shipping Address: &address;
  </shipping_address>
  <shipping_city>Shipping City: &city;
  </shipping_city>
  <shipping_state>Shipping State: &state;
  </shipping_state>
  <shipping_zip>Shipping Zip Code: &zip;
  </shipping_zip>
  &description;
</business>
```

a. Create the `description.xml` file as referenced by the `description` entity.

b. Open the `business.xml` document in Internet Explorer and verify that your external entity in the `description.xml` file is being parsed correctly.

c. Create a file called `shipping_address.xml` that contains the XML code for the shipping information: address, city, state, and zip.

d. Replace the entities for the shipping information in your `business.xml` document—address, city, state, and zip—with this one external entity reference to the file that now contains the information.

e. Open your new `business.xml` document in Internet Explorer. What is displayed in Internet Explorer should look exactly the same as it did in step b.

CHAPTER THREE

Describing XML Documents with DTDs and XML Schemas

As you will learn in this chapter, document models allow XML document authors to assign rules to the way their documents are structured. Using a document model, you can enforce rules, such as requiring certain elements and attributes and even limiting the types of data a document can contain. Document models allow for the creation of document standards within a particular XML vocabulary.

Chapter Objectives

- To learn what a document model is and what you can do with it
- To understand the differences between a validating and a nonvalidating parser
- To learn how to write and use a DTD with an XML document
- To learn about the new XML schema specification for XML

Using a Document Model: DTDs and Schemas

In Chapter Two, you learned about the syntax rules and components that make up the XML 1.0 specification. You also learned how to create well-formed XML documents and how to use a nonvalidating parser to check the syntax of documents to ensure that they are well formed. In this chapter, you will learn how to add rules to your XML documents that enforce structure by using a document model such as a document type definition (DTD) or XML schema.

A document model defines the vocabulary and grammar rules for a particular markup language. Documents that are correct according to the rules of a document model are said to be **valid**. Here are examples of what you can do using a document model:

- Define the elements your document can contain
- Define the order in which the elements appear
- Require that certain elements appear
- Define the allowed number of occurrences of a given element
- Define the type of data an element can contain
- Define child elements for a given element
- Define the attributes for each of your elements
- Assign constraints to the attribute values

Document models are not required by XML and may not be needed. Whether to create a document model for a particular application is up to the XML author and depends on who or what types of program will use the information. If you want to share your XML documents with other people or programs, using a document model can be crucial. For a document to be shared, all the programs that use it must agree on the format and must understand the types of information to expect within it. A document model specifies that format and information.

The XML components that you learned about in Chapter Two are the building blocks of the language—analogous to the nouns and adjectives of English. A document's **structure** defines how these pieces fit together to form a cohesive document, much as a collection of sentences fits together to form a paragraph.

This paragraph that you are reading right now is made up of four complete sentences. Each sentence is correct in syntax and is considered valid based on the rules of English. However, these sentences wouldn't make sense if they were read out of order or out of context, or if they did not relate to one another in content. Although each sentence may be syntactically correct, a paragraph that has no structure—one whose sentences are not somehow related—does not make sense and therefore has no real value for readers.

More than likely, you deal with structured documents every day. Examples of structured documents include company letterhead, memos, e-mail messages, invoices, legal contracts, programs, and various forms. We expect to see certain items in certain documents. For example, if you make a purchase, you expect the invoice to show an itemized list of your purchases and a total sale amount. Imagine an XML document for an invoice that does not have any rules for its structure:

```
<?xml version="1.0"?>
<invoice>
   <merchant_name>Acme Shoe Shoppe</merchant_name>
   <flower_name>Lilly</flower_name>
   <ingredient_list>
      <ingredient amount="1 cup">Milk</ingredient>
      <ingredient amount="3 teaspoons">Butter</ingredient>
      <ingredient amount="2 teaspoons">Salt</ingredient>
      <ingredient amount="3 cloves">Garlic</ingredient>
      </ingredient_list>
   <birthday date="May 7"/>
</invoice>
```

Although the XML syntax of this document is correct and a nonvalidating parser would happily pass it through without any errors, these elements and attributes do not make sense for an invoice document. This information is not useful to either the buyer or the merchant.

Now let's look at a structured invoice document:

```
<?xml version="1.0"?>
<invoice>
   <merchant_name>Acme Shoe Shoppe</merchant_name>
      <merchant_address>
      <street>123 Main Street</street>
      <city>Lancaster</city>
      <state>OH</state>
      <zip>43031</zip>
   </merchant_address>
   <sale_date date="03-07-01"/>
   <items_purchased>
      <item price="34.00" quantity="1">Sneakers</item>
      <item price="5.00" quantity="1">White Socks</item>
   </items_purchased>
   <total_sale>39.00</total_sale>
   <payment type="cash"/>
   <message>Thank you for shopping at Acme Shoe Shoppe</message>
</invoice>
```

This document makes more sense because it contains elements and attributes related to an invoice. Again, both of these examples are well-formed and valid XML documents, but the second one would be much more useful to a program that, for example, calculated total sales or tracked inventory.

This chapter covers the syntax and format of DTDs and provides an overview of XML schemas. But first let's take a quick look at validating parsers, which you must use to check documents that use DTDs.

Using a Validating Parser

In Chapter Two, you learned about nonvalidating parsers, which can be used to check the syntax of an XML document to determine whether it is well formed. To check a document against a DTD, however, you must use a validating parser.

The default XML parser that ships with Internet Explorer is not a validating parser and will not tell you whether you have errors in your DTD. Microsoft provides validating parsers free of charge at the following Web site:

```
http://msdn.microsoft.com/downloads/samples/internet/xml/
xml_validator
```

☆ **SHORTCUT** This chapter uses a validating parser from Microsoft's Web site to validate the examples. You may want to download this parser and validate the examples as we go along. Follow these steps:

1. In a browser, go to the Microsoft parsers Web site and follow the instructions.
2. Open the page from your hard drive in Internet Explorer.
3. In the box labeled Enter a URL to Load, type the path to the document that you would like to validate.
4. Locate the Validate button toward the bottom of the screen. Press this button to validate your document.

☆ **WARNING** DTDs are not required in XML, and you can use a non-validating parser to check an XML document that does not have an associated DTD. However, some validating parser requires a DTD to validate the document against and will produce an error if it does not find one.The validating parser from Microsoft that we use in this chapter will allow you to parse documents without DTDs without producing error messages.

Let's look at an example. Below is a small XML document that does not have a DTD associated with it:

```
<?xml version="1.0"?>
<invoice>
    The total of this invoice is $39.00
</invoice>
```

Figure 3.1 shows this document in Internet Explorer using the non-validating parser that comes with the browser, and Figure 3.2 shows this document using the validating parser from Microsoft.

Notice that the validating parser will parse this document with no errors even though it does not have a DTD associated with it. The validating parser also does not show the XML code like the non-validating parser does, it simply states whether or not the document is well-formed and valid.

Figure 3.1 XML Document without DTD Using Non-Validating Parser in Internet Explorer

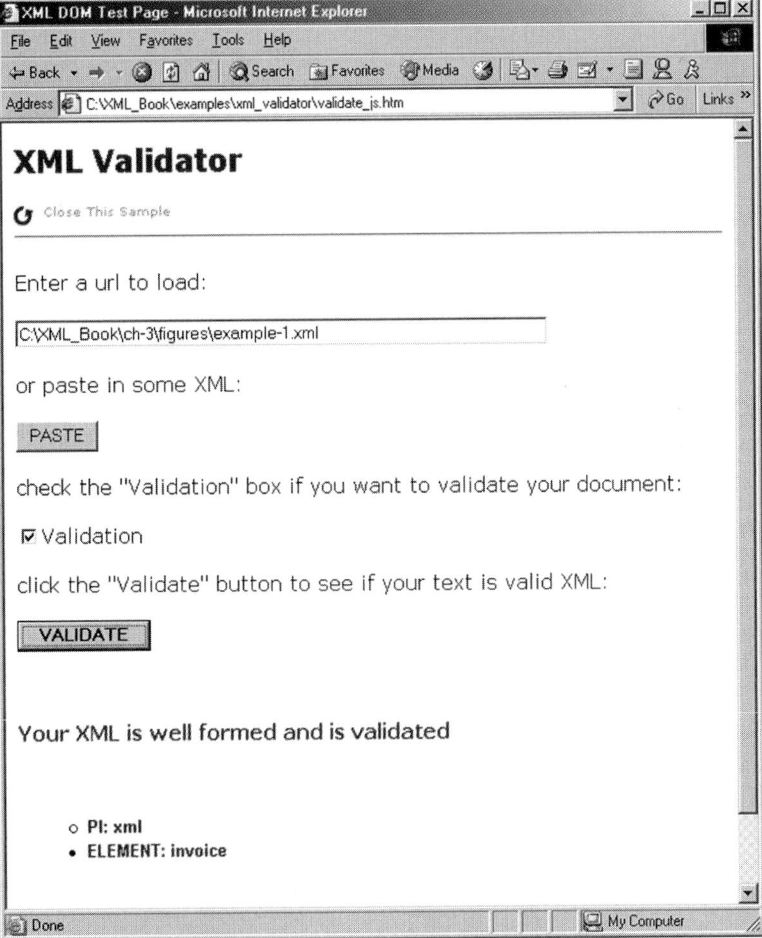

Figure 3.2 XML Document without DTD Using Validating Parser from Microsoft

Now, let's add a DTD to our document (don't worry if you do not understand the syntax, we will cover this later in the chapter) :

```
1   <?xml version="1.0"?>
2   <!DOCTYPE invoice [
3       <!ELEMENT invoice    (#PCDATA)>
4   ]>
5   <invoice>
6       The total of this invoice is $39.00
7   </invoice>
```

This is the DTD for the document

In this example, the DTD is on lines 2–4. Our document only contains one element, `<invoice>`, which is declared on line 3 (again, don't worry about the syntax, you will learn this later in the chapter. The important thing to note is that the name of the element being declared is "invoice"). Figure 3.3 shows this document using the validating parser.

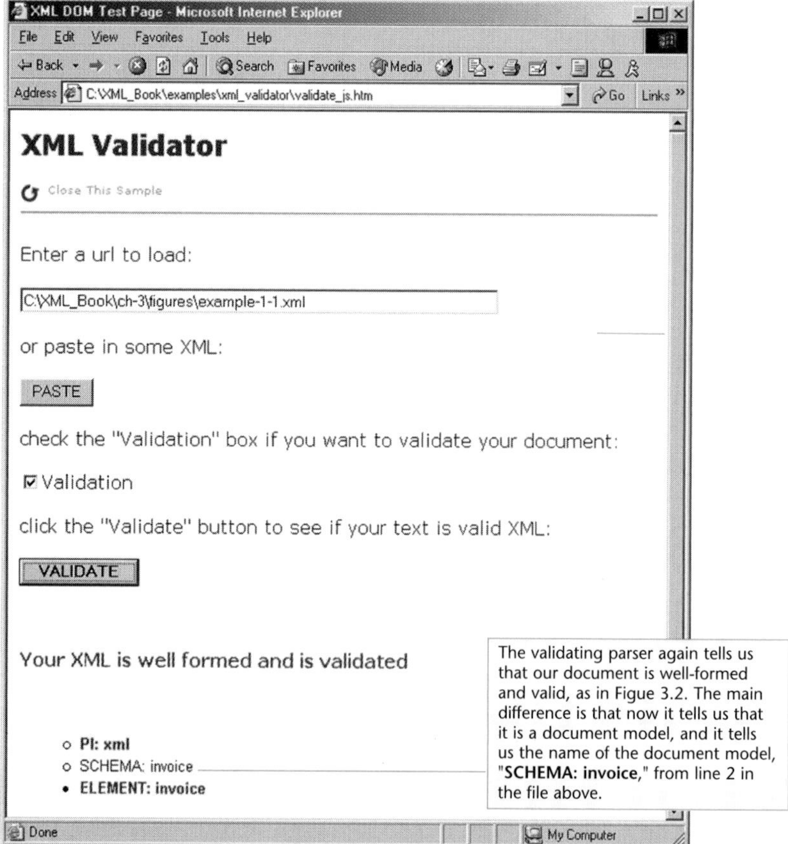

Figure 3.3 XML Document with DTD Using Validating Parser from Microsoft

To demonstrate how the validating parser works to validate documents against DTDs, let's change the element declaration on line 3 to declare an element called memo instead of invoice:

```
1    <?xml version="1.0"?>
2    <!DOCTYPE invoice [
3        <!ELEMENT memo (#PCDATA)>
4    ]>
5    <invoice>
6        The total of this invoice is $39.00
7    </invoice>
```

Change invoice to memo

Now, let's validate this document. Figure 3.4 shows this document in Microsoft's validating parser. Notice that now the validating parser produces an error message stating that "The element 'invoice' is used but not declared in the DTD/Schema." This is because we changed the name of the element from <invoice> to <memo>. In order to use an element in a document that has a DTD, that element must be declared.

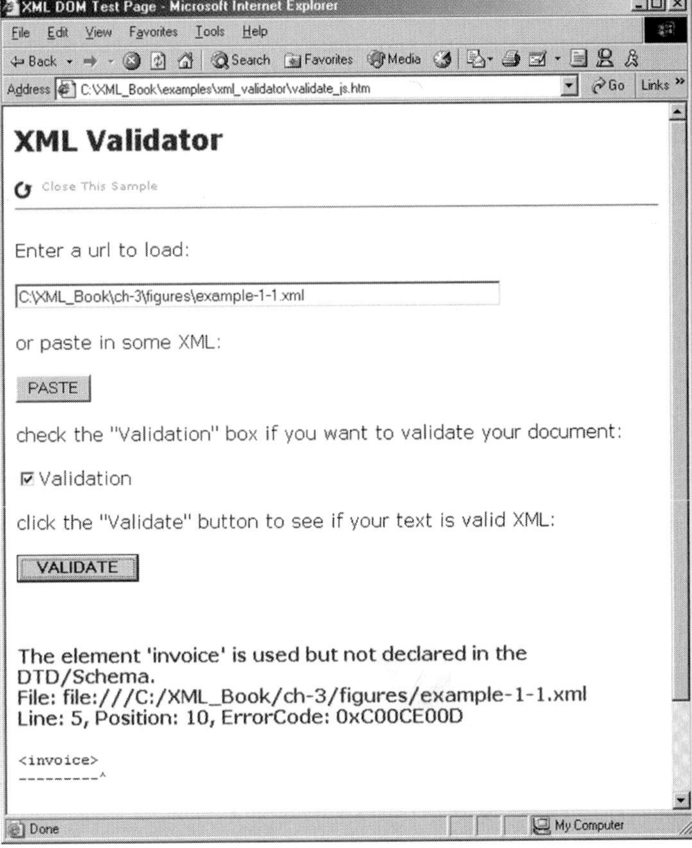

Figure 3.4 XML Document with DTD Error Using Validating Parser from Microsoft

However, even though a validating parser will produce an error message if there are errors in the DTD, a non-validating parser will *not* produce an error message. Figure 3.5 shows this same document with the error in the DTD in Internet Explorer's non-validating parser.

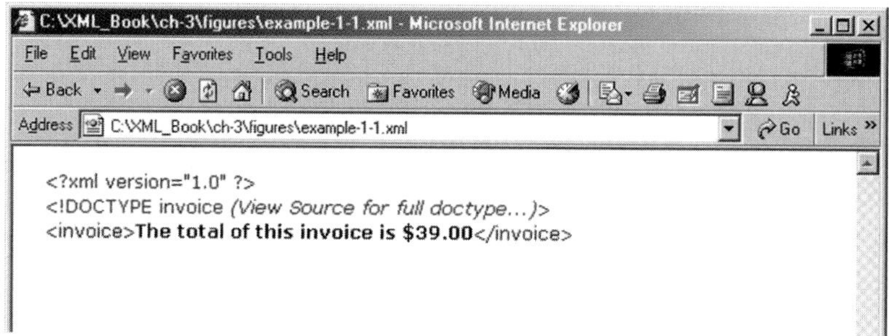

Figure 3.5 XML Document with DTD Error Using Internet Explorer's Non-Validating Parser

☆**TIP** The concept of validating vs. non-validating parsers discussed in this section may be confusing. The rest of this chapter explains DTD's in detail. If you had trouble following the example in this section, read the rest of the chapter to gain a better understanding of DTD syntax and how they work, and then come back and re-read this section.

The non-validating parser displays the document just fine, and does not produce any errors concerning the errors in the DTD. That is because, as stated earlier, non-validating parsers do not validate documents against a document model. As long as the document follows all of the syntax rules, and is well-formed, the non-validating parser will not produce any error messages.

Overview of DTDs

You learned in Chapter One that XML is a metalanguage that is used to create markup languages. DTDs are one of the XML mechanisms that allow you to structure these languages. HTML is one example of a markup language with a defined set of elements. The URL for the HTML 4.01 DTD is:

```
http://www.w3.org/TR/html401/sgml/dtd.html
```

Each HTML element and any associated attributes are clearly defined in the DTD. Applications that process HTML documents, such as Web browsers, use the DTD to determine how to display or handle the various elements. If an HTML programmer uses elements or tags that are not defined in the DTD, the browser will not know how to process them because it does not recognize them as part of the DTD. Unlike HTML, however, XML is extensible, and this means that if you write a DTD for your XML language or program, people who use your DTD can extend it if necessary to meet their needs.

SHORTCUT DTDs are widely used, and you can download a variety of free public DTDs. For more information, see "Online References" at the end of the chapter.

There are two kinds of DTD declarations:

- Internal DTD subset: provided as part of the document
- External DTD subset: provided as an external file

The syntax and rules for defining the pieces of a DTD are the same whether they are internal or external. Let's look at internal subsets first, and then we'll see how to make the necessary modifications to use an external DTD.

Element Declarations

If you are using a DTD with your XML document, the DTD must declare all elements used in the document. Otherwise, the parser will produce an error, as we saw in the last section. Following is the syntax for declaring an element in a DTD:

```
<!ELEMENT  element_name (content model)>
```

An element declaration begins with `<!ELEMENT`, followed by the name of the element, followed by the type of data the element can contain. The latter is called its content model, which you will learn about in the next section.

Following is a sample XML document with an internal DTD declaration:

```
1 <?xml version="1.0" standalone="yes"?>
2 <!DOCTYPE email [
3       <!ELEMENT email      (#PCDATA)>
4 ]>
5 <email>
6       This is my e-mail message
7 </email>
```

Internal DTD

TIP DTDs are part of what is known as the document prolog in XML. The **document prolog** is the set of declarations—including the XML declaration, document model declarations, stylesheet declarations, and so on—that appear before the line containing the root element. In the example here, lines 1 through 4 make up the document prolog. In later chapters you will learn about other declarations that are part of the document prolog.

Let's look at each line in detail:

- Line 1 of this document is the XML declaration, which you learned about in Chapter Two. The `standalone` attribute tells the processor that this document contains within itself all the data needed and not to look for any external files for additional declarations.
- Line 2 is the `DOCTYPE` declaration, which consists of an opening `<!`, followed by the keyword `DOCTYPE`, followed by the name of the root element and a `[` character, which opens the DTD subset. This line opens the DTD.

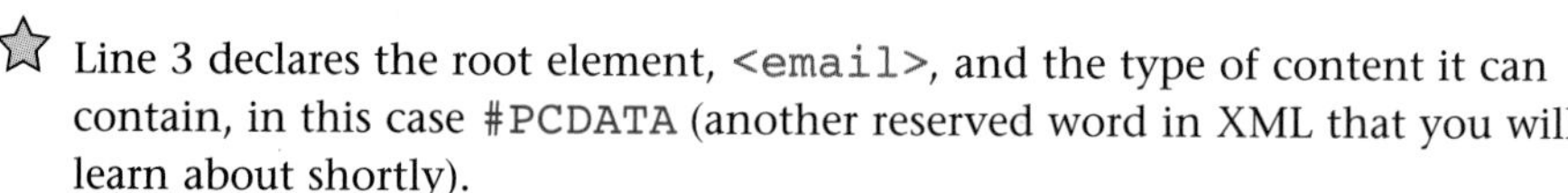

- Line 3 declares the root element, <email>, and the type of content it can contain, in this case #PCDATA (another reserved word in XML that you will learn about shortly).
- Line 4 contains the characters]>, which end the DTD. The DTD data is contained between the opening [character and the ending] character. So in this example, the entire DTD declaration starts on line 2 and ends on line 4 and contains a declaration for only one element, <email>.
- Lines 5 through 7 are the complete XML document.

WARNING DOCTYPE is a reserved keyword in XML. It is used for declarations and must always appear in uppercase letters.

Content Model for Elements

The rules that define the type of content an element can contain are known as the element's **content model**. Content models are associated with elements and follow the name of the element in the element declaration. Table 3.1 summarizes the content model types for elements.

Table 3.1 Content Model Types for XML Elements

Content Model	Declaration Syntax	Description
Text	<!ELEMENT invoice (#PCDATA)>	Text or character data.
Elements	<!ELEMENT invoice (element_name)>	Content that consists of other elements.
Mixed content	<!ELEMENT invoice (#PCDATA, element_name)>	Contains both text content and other elements. The #PCDATA declaration must appear first.
EMPTY	<!ELEMENT invoice EMPTY>	Empty element that contains no content.
ANY	<!ELEMENT invoice ANY>	Can contain text or elements.

Let's look at an example. The following XML document can be used to describe e-mail messages:

```
<?xml version="1.0" standalone="yes"?>
<emails>
    <message>
       <to>joe&#64;acmeshipping.com</to>
       <from>brenda&#64;xyzcompany.com</from>
       <date_sent/>
       <subject>Order 10011</subject>
       <body>
          Joe,
          Please let me know if order number 10011 has shipped.
          Thanks,
          Brenda
       </body>
    </message>
</emails>
```

Note: The "@" character in the e-mail addresses—`joe@acmeshipping.com` and `brenda@xyzcompany.com`—has been replaced by the character entity value `@`.

Here is the internal DTD for this document:

```
1 <!DOCTYPE    emails  [
2     <!ELEMENT emails      (message)>
3     <!ELEMENT message     (to, from, date_sent, subject, body) >
4     <!ELEMENT to          (#PCDATA) >
5     <!ELEMENT from        (#PCDATA) >
6     <!ELEMENT date_sent   EMPTY>
7     <!ELEMENT subject     (#PCDATA) >
8     <!ELEMENT body        ANY>
9  ]>
```

☆ **TIP** The code examples in this chapter include extra spacing between the words to make the code easier to read. This is a common practice used by people who write code to help other people who look at their code to understand it better. XML parsers do not require this spacing. A parser will ignore extra space in an XML file.

Now let's look at it line by line.

- Line 1 is the internal DTD declaration.
- Line 2 defines the `<emails>` root element and states that it contains one `<message>` element.
- Line 3 defines the list of elements that `<message>` contains and the order in which they must appear. In this case, all elements are required.
- Line 4 defines the element `<to>` to contain character data (text).
- Line 5 defines the element `<from>` to contain character data (text).
- Line 6 defines the element `<date_sent>` as an empty element.

- Line 7 defines the element <subject> to contain character data (text).
- Line 8 defines the element <body> to contain any kind of content. This means that it can contain text or other elements. This declaration allows for more flexibility. For example, declaring the content model as **ANY** would allow the sender of the message to include an element called <order_num> in the body of the message. If the content model had been declared as #PCDATA, the following would result in an error:

```
<body>
   Joe,
   Please let me know if order number
       <order_num>10011</order_num>
   has shipped.
   Thanks,
   Brenda
</body>
```

This would cause an error if the content model for <body> was #PCDATA.

- Line 9 ends the DTD declarations.

Putting it all together, here is what the complete XML document would look like with the internal DTD:

```
<?xml version="1.0" standalone="yes"?>
<!DOCTYPE emails [
   <!ELEMENT emails      (message)>
   <!ELEMENT message     (to, from, date_sent, subject, body)>
   <!ELEMENT to          (#PCDATA)>
   <!ELEMENT from        (#PCDATA)>
   <!ELEMENT date_sent   EMPTY>
   <!ELEMENT subject     (#PCDATA)>
   <!ELEMENT body        ANY>
]>
<emails>
   <message>
      <to>joe&#64;acmeshipping.com</to>
      <from>brenda&#64;xyzcompany.com</from>
      <date_sent/>
      <subject>Order 10011</subject>
      <body>
         Joe,
         Please let me know if order number 10011 has shipped.
         Thanks,
         Brenda
      </body>
   </message>
</emails>
```

Figure 3.6 shows the well-formed document in Internet Explorer, and Figure 3.7 shows this example using a validating parser. The validating parser shows that the sample document is well formed and valid. Notice that the validating parser does not show the actual XML document, but lists the name of the DTD, "SCHEMA: emails" and the element name, "ELEMENT: emails" in the document at the bottom of the page.

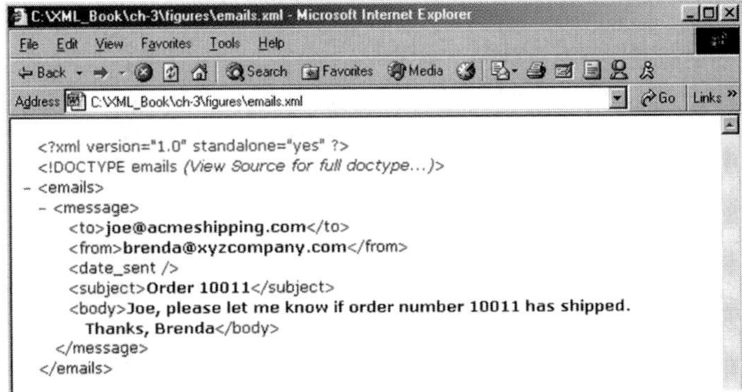

C:\XML_Book\ch-3\figures\emails.xml - Microsoft Internet Explorer
File Edit View Favorites Tools Help
Back Search Favorites Media
Address C:\XML_Book\ch-3\figures\emails.xml
Go Links
<?xml version="1.0" standalone="yes" ?>
<!DOCTYPE emails (View Source for full doctype...)>
- <emails>
- <message>
<to>joe@acmeshipping.com</to>
<from>brenda@xyzcompany.com</from>
<date_sent />
<subject>Order 10011</subject>
<body>Joe, please let me know if order number 10011 has shipped. Thanks, Brenda</body>
</message>
</emails>

Figure 3.6 Well-Formed XML Document Using Internet Explorer's Non-Validating Parser

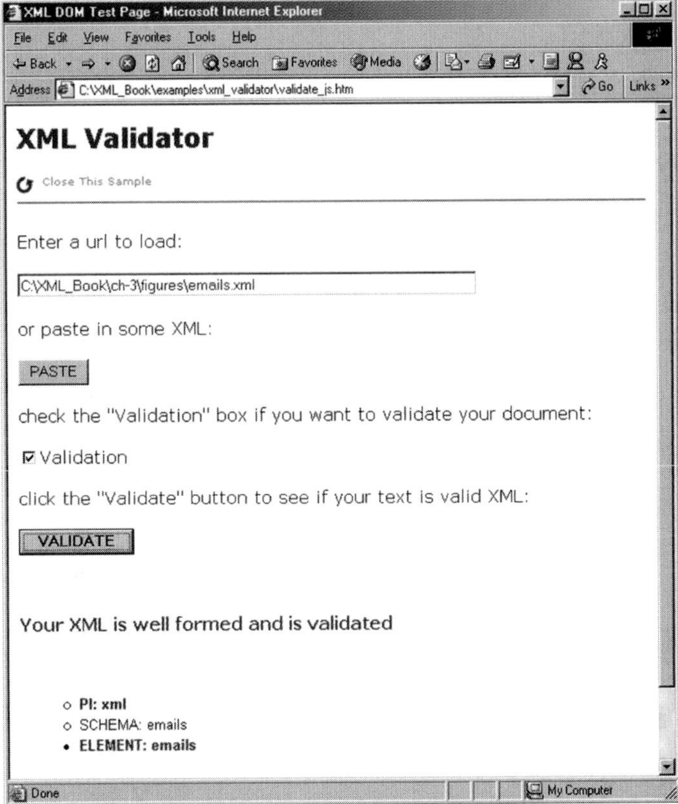

Figure 3.7 Valid XML Document Using Microsoft's Validating Parser

Character Notations

So far, all the elements in these examples have been required, and the documents have required exactly one occurrence of each element. But what if you are not sure whether an element will exist in a document, or you are not sure how many times it will occur? XML provides special character notations that allow you to be more flexible with elements. Table 3.2 defines these special character notations and explains how they are used.

Table 3.2 Special Character Notations

Character	Syntax	Description
?	`message?`	Question mark: indicates that the element or value may occur zero or exactly one time.
*	`message*`	Asterisk: indicates that the element or value may occur zero or more times.
+	`message+`	Plus: indicates that the element or value may occur one or many times. Compared with the ? or *, the + requires that the element or value occur at least once.
|	`(x|y|z)`	Vertical bar: used as an "or" operator in a list of values and means that only one of the items in the list can be set as the value.
( )	`(x,y,z)`	Parentheses: used to indicate a set of values.
,	`(x,y,z)`	Comma: indicates sequence. Elements separated by commas must appear in the order specified.

Attributes

After you declare all your elements, you declare any attributes for them. **Attribute** declarations give you control over the values of attributes in a document and determine whether each attribute is required. Following is the syntax for declaring attributes:

```
<!ATTLIST element_name
    attribute_name-1          data_type     default_value
    attribute_name-2          data_type     default_value
    attribute_name-3          data_type     default_value>
```

The `ATTLIST` keyword begins the declaration, followed by the name of the element, followed by the list of attributes. Each attribute declaration consists of the name of the attribute, the type of data that the attribute value should be (known as the attribute's "data type"), and the default value or usage for the attribute. Tables 3.3 and 3.4 describe the default value options and data types for attributes.

Table 3.3 Default Values for Attributes

Attribute Type	Description
`#FIXED`	Value for the attribute is fixed. The value of the attribute must match the value assigned in the DTD.
`#REQUIRED`	This attribute is required. The element must contain the attribute, and it must have a value to be valid.
`#IMPLIED`	This attribute is optional. The element may or may not contain this attribute. It can be omitted and still be valid.

Table 3.4 Data Types for Attributes

Attribute Type	Description
`CDATA`	Character data: can include character and general entities. Cannot include other elements.
`ID`	Unique identifier: used to give an element a unique label within a document. This attribute value verifies that no two elements have the same value for this attribute. Must start with a letter.
`IDREF`	Identifier reference: used to identify ID labels. If the IDREF references a value that is not specified by an ID in the document, it will produce an error.
`IDREFS`	Identifier references: like IDREF but used to identify two or more ID references within a document separated by spaces. As with IDREF, all the IDs must exist in the document.
`ENTITY`	General entity: assigns an external entity name as the value of the attribute.
`ENTITIES`	General entities: like ENTITY but references two or more external entity references separated by spaces.
`NMTOKEN`	Name token: string of character data that can consist of letters, numbers, hyphens, periods, underscores, and colons. Cannot contain white space.
`NMTOKENS`	Name tokens: like NMTOKEN but references a list of tokens separated by spaces.
Enumerated List	List of all possible values for an attribute separated by the pipe ("|") character. The attribute must be one of these values.

Let's modify the e-mail document to add a few attributes:

```
<?xml version="1.0" standalone="yes"?>
<emails>
   <message num="a1" to="joe&#64;acmeshipping.com"
      from="brenda&#64;xyzcompany.com" date="02/09/01">
      <subject title="Order 10011"/>
      <body>
         Joe,
         Please let me know if order number 10011 has shipped.
         Thanks,
         Brenda
      </body>
      <reply status="yes"/>
   </message>
</emails>
```

Added attributes

The example now defines `num`, `to`, `from`, and `date` as attributes for the `<message>` element, `title` as an attribute for the `<subject>` element and `status` as an attribute for the `<reply>` element. Following is the DTD for this document and a line-by-line description of the various components:

```
1  <!DOCTYPE           emails  [
2      <!ELEMENT       emails      (message+)>
3      <!ELEMENT       message     (subject?, body, reply*)>
4         <!ATTLIST    message
5                      num         ID          #REQUIRED
6                      to          CDATA       #REQUIRED
7                      from        CDATA       #FIXED "brenda&#64;
                                               xyzcompany.com"
8                      date        CDATA       #REQUIRED>
9      <!ELEMENT       subject     EMPTY>
10        <!ATTLIST    subject
11                     title       CDATA       #IMPLIED>
12     <!ELEMENT       body                    ANY>
13     <!ELEMENT       reply                   EMPTY>
14        <!ATTLIST    reply
15           status     (yes | no)             "no">
16 ]>
```

- ☆ Line 1 is the internal DTD declaration.
- ☆ Line 2 defines `<emails>` as the root element and states that it must contain at least one, but can contain many, `<message>` elements, as indicated by the + character.

- Line 3 defines the list of elements that <message> contains and the order in which they must appear. The <subject> element is optional and can occur zero or exactly one time, as indicated by the ? character. The <body> element must occur, and must occur only once. The reply attribute can occur zero or many times, as indicated by the * character.
- Line 4 begins the ATTLIST declaration, which defines the attributes for the <message> element. Each of the three attributes—to, from, and date—is defined with its data type.
- Line 5 defines the num attribute for the <message> element to be of type ID. The value assigned to this attribute must be unique.
- Line 6 defines the to attribute for the <message> element to be a CDATA type, meaning that it can contain character data and is required.
- Line 7 defines the from attribute for the <message> element to be a CDATA type, and the value of this attribute is fixed. This means that if anyone other than brenda@xyzcompany.com is given as the value of this attribute, the validating parser will produce an error.
- Line 8 defines the date attribute for the <message> element and ends the ATTLIST declaration.
- Line 9 defines the <subject> element as an empty element.
- Line 10 begins the ATTLIST declaration for the <subject> element.
- Line 11 defines the attribute title for the <subject> element and ends the ATTLIST declaration. This attribute is defined as of CDATA type and is #IMPLIED, which means that it is optional. If the <subject> element has no title attribute assigned, the document will still be valid.
- Line 12 defines the <body> element with a content model of ANY, meaning that it can contain any kind of content.
- Line 13 defines the <reply> element as an empty element.
- Line 14 begins the ATTLIST declaration for the <reply> element.
- Line 15 defines the attribute status for the <reply> element. The value is an enumerated list of values: (yes | no). This means that the value can be either yes or no, as indicated by the "|" character. The default value is no, as indicated in the declaration.
- Line 16 ends the DTD declarations.

Here is the complete XML document:

```
<?xml version="1.0" standalone="yes"?>
<!DOCTYPE             emails [
   <!ELEMENT          emails     (message+)>
   <!ELEMENT          message    (subject?, body, reply*)>
      <!ATTLIST       message
                      num        ID       #REQUIRED
                      to         CDATA    #REQUIRED
                      from       CDATA    #FIXED "brenda&#64;
                                          xyzcompany.com"
                      date       CDATA    #REQUIRED>
      <!ELEMENT       subject             EMPTY>
      <!ATTLIST       subject
                      title      CDATA    #IMPLIED>
   <!ELEMENT          body                ANY>
   <!ELEMENT          reply               EMPTY>
      <!ATTLIST       reply
                      status     (yes | no)    "no">
]>
<emails>
   <message num="a1" to="joe&#64;acmeshipping.com"
      from="brenda&#64;xyzcompany.com" date="02/09/01">
      <subject title="Order 10011"/>
      <body>
         Joe,
         Please let me know if order number 10011 has shipped.
         Thanks,
         Brenda
      </body>
      <reply status="yes"/>
   </message>
</emails>
```

Figure 3.8 shows the well-formed document in Internet Explorer's non-validating parser. Validating this document in Microsoft's validating parser would produce the same output as Figure 3.4, shown earlier. The parser shows that the document is well formed and valid.

Comments

Comments in DTDs are written the same way as for XML documents:

```
<!-- This is a comment to be used in a DTD -->
```

Comments can be used anywhere in a DTD and are ignored by the parser. Use comments to label sections of your DTD, to clarify usage, or to communicate with others working on the DTD document.

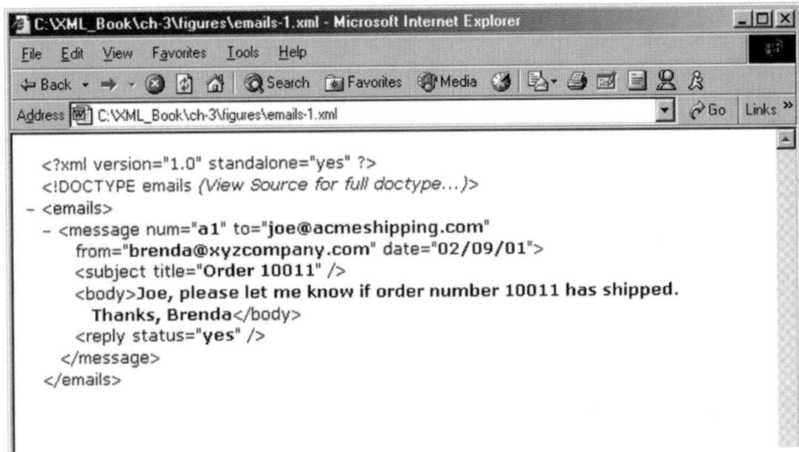

Figure 3.8 Well-Formed XML Document

External DTDs

The earlier examples contain internal DTDs, meaning that all the element and attribute declarations are declared inside the XML document. The `standalone` attribute of the XML declaration is set to `yes` to indicate that all the information needed for these documents is located within the document.

To declare a DTD as an external file, you first set the `standalone` value in the XML declaration to `no` to tell the validating parser that it will need to look outside the current XML document for the DTD:

```
<?xml version="1.0" standalone="no"?>
```

The external DTD declaration must tell the parser where to find the DTD file:

```
<!DOCTYPE emails SYSTEM "emails.dtd">
```

As with internal DTDs, the declaration starts with `<!DOCTYPE`, followed by the name of the element. It then uses the keyword **`SYSTEM`** to tell the parser that the DTD is external. The last piece of information is the location of the DTD file. The file can be on the local system, or it can reside anywhere on the Internet. The declaration for a DTD located on a remote system on the Internet would look like this:

```
<!DOCTYPE emails SYSTEM "http://www.acme.com/emails.dtd">
```

The syntax of an external DTD, and the declarations, are exactly the same as for an internal DTD. You can modify the earlier example to place the DTD information in a separate file. Figure 3.9 shows the XML document with the external DTD declaration, and Figure 3.10 shows the corresponding external DTD file.

```
<?xml version="1.0" standalone="no"?>
<!DOCTYPE emails SYSTEM "emails.dtd">
<emails>
    <message num="a1"
             to="joe&#64;acmeshipping.com"
             from="brenda&#64;xyzcompany.com"
             date="02/09/01">
    <subject title="Order 10011" />
    <body>
          Joe,
          Please let me know if order number
          10011 has shipped.
          Thanks,
          Brenda
    </body>
    <reply status="yes"/>
    </message>
</emails>
```

Figure 3.9 XML Document `emails.xml`

```
<!ELEMENT   emails     (message+)>
<!ELEMENT   message    (subject?, body, reply*)>
   <!ATTLIST message
   num       ID              #REQUIRED
   to        CDATA           #REQUIRED
    from     CDATA           #FIXED
             "brenda&#64;xyzcompany.com"
   date      CDATA           #REQUIRED>
<!ELEMENT   subject          EMPTY>
   <!ATTLIST  subject
   title     CDATA           #IMPLIED>
<!ELEMENT   body             ANY>
<!ELEMENT   reply            EMPTY>
   <!ATTLIST reply
   status   (yes | no) "no">
```

Figure 3.10 External DTD File `emails.dtd`

☆ **SHORTCUT** To try this example yourself, use a text editor to create the two files in Figures 3.9 and 3.10, and save them as `emails.xml` and `emails.dtd`. Be sure to save both files in the same directory. Then validate them in the Internet Explorer validating parser, as discussed earlier in the chapter.

Public DTDs

Many DTDs have been written and are publicly available for you to use. Some public DTDs have been defined as standards by the ISO (International Organization for Standardization). "Online References" at the end of this chapter shows the URL of the ISO Web site.

The declaration for a public DTD is similar to that of an external DTD but uses the keyword `PUBLIC`. The following sample declaration includes the public XHTML DTD in your document:

```
<!DOCTYPE html PUBLIC "-//W3C//DTD XHTML 1.0 STRICT//EN"
"DTD/http://www.w3c.org/DTD/xhtml1-strict.dtd">
```

Using Both Internal and External DTDs

A document can contain both internal and external DTD declarations. If an element declaration appears in both the internal and the external DTD, the internal declaration overrides the external. This allows you to customize a public or external DTD for your own use if you need to change the behavior of only a few elements. For example, if you wanted to use the DTD from the earlier example, **`emails.dtd`**, but modify the attribute `title` for the `<subject>` element to be required (instead of optional), you could override the external DTD with an internal declaration:

```
<?xml version="1.0" standalone="no"?>
<!DOCTYPE emails SYSTEM "emails.dtd" [
    <!ELEMENT   subject         EMPTY>
        <!ATTLIST subject
            title CDATA         #REQUIRED>
]>
```

You could also use the internal DTD to extend the external DTD to include additional elements and to declare any entities the document may use in the internal declaration section.

Overview of XML Schemas

The W3C released the XML Schema Language recommendation in May 2001. The recommendation contains two parts: Part 1 covers structure, and Part 2 covers data types. The XML schema was developed as an alternative to DTDs and offers a more powerful method to describe and set constraints on XML components.

Following is a list of enhancements that an XML schema provides over DTDs:

- Instead of stating that an element or attribute can contain text characters, a schema allows you to match string patterns within the content.
- It provides more data types, including Booleans, numbers, dates, and times. It also allows you to define your own data types.

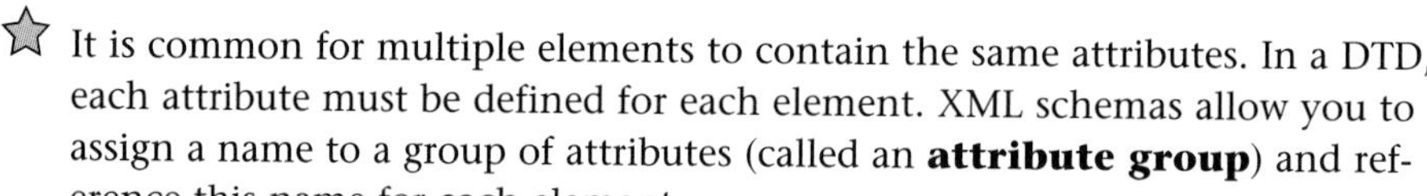

- It is common for multiple elements to contain the same attributes. In a DTD, each attribute must be defined for each element. XML schemas allow you to assign a name to a group of attributes (called an **attribute group**) and reference this name for each element.
- It supports namespaces, which you will learn about in Chapter Five. DTDs do not support namespaces.
- Because schemas are written in XML, a standard XML parser can be used to check whether schema documents are well formed.

Schemas are gaining popularity now that the final specification has been released, and they will probably replace DTDs for many projects. However, because the specification is new, few tools have been written to work specifically with schema documents.

XML schemas rely heavily on XML namespaces, which you will learn about in Chapter Five. Chapter Seven provides some examples of XML schemas.

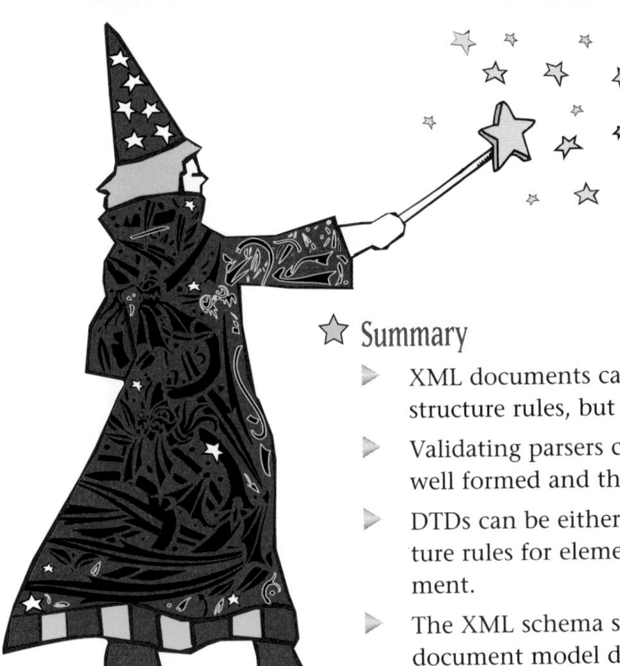

Summary

- XML documents can use a document model to provide structure rules, but it is not required.
- Validating parsers check a document to ensure that it is well formed and that it adheres to its associated DTD.
- DTDs can be either internal or external. They define structure rules for elements and attributes in an XML document.
- The XML schema specification promises to add features to document model declarations.

Online References

W3C XML 1.0 Specification (Second Edition)
`http://www.w3.org/TR/REC-xml`

W3C XML Schema
`http://www.w3.org/XML/Schema`

XML Schemas Cover Pages
`http://xml.coverpages.org/schemas.html`

Microsoft's Validating Parser Site
`http://msdn.microsoft.com/downloads/samples/internet/xml/xml_validator`

Webreview: DTDs
`http://www.WebReview.com/2000/08_11/developers/08_11_00_2.shtml`

The DocBook DTD and Project Information
`http://nwalsh.com/docbook/index.html`

DTD Repository for HTML
`http://www.ict.nsc.ru/docs/html/web_techs_html_repository.html`

International Organization for Standardization
`http://www.iso.org`

☆Review Questions

1. Describe the difference between syntax and structure in an XML document.
2. What is the difference between a validating and a nonvalidating parser?
3. Describe what the `standalone` attribute in the XML declaration does.
4. Describe two content models for elements.
5. What does the + character notation mean?
6. How do you declare an attribute that is optional?
7. If an element is declared in both the external and the internal DTD, which declaration takes precedence?
8. Where are entity declarations placed—in the internal or the external DTD?
9. Describe two advantages of XML schemas compared with DTDs.

☆Hands-On Exercises

1. The following XML document causes an error when parsed with Microsoft's validating parser. There are three errors in the DTD. Fix them so that the document is valid.

```
<?xml version="1.0" standalone="yes"?>
<!DOCTYPE    message_list
   <!ELEMENT messages          (message)>
   <!ELEMENT message           (body, subject)>
   <!ELEMENT subject           (PCDATA)>
   <!ELEMENT body              ANY>
]>
<message_list>
   <message>
      <subject>Reminder</subject>
      <body>
         Remember to pick up milk on the way home.
      </body>
   </message>
</message_list>
```

2. Create an internal DTD for the following XML document. Create an enumerated type for the `class_day` attribute, and define the data type for the `id` attribute to ID. Assume that all attributes are required:

```
<?xml version="1.0" standalone="yes"?>
<course_list>
   <course id="bw101" class_day="Tuesday"
   class_time="3:00">
      <title>Introduction to Basket Weaving</title>
      <instructor>Judy Flowers</instructor>
      <description>Learn how to weave straw baskets
      </description>
   </course>
</course_list>
```

3. For the example in Exercise 2, assign a `FIXED` value of to the `class_day` attribute.
4. Create the DTD for the XML document in Exercise 2 as an external DTD.
5. Test your answers from Exercises 2, 3, and 4 in a validating parser.

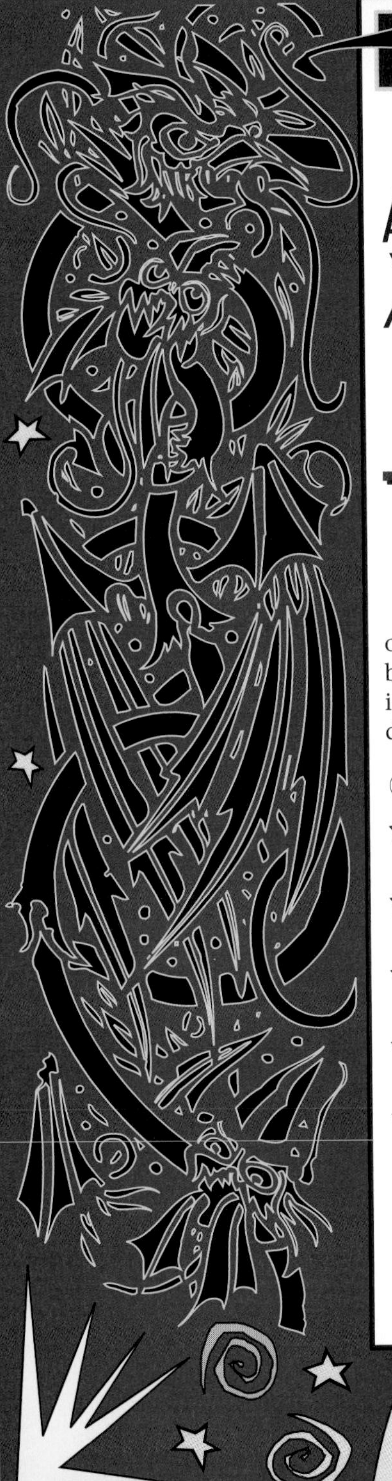

CHAPTER FOUR

All About Style: XML Presentation

This chapter explains how to use style sheets to create the end product: a well-formed and well-formatted XML document. You use style sheets to format the output of an XML processing program. You will use a Web browser as the primary output destination for the examples in this chapter, but you can create style sheets to format your documents for many types of output.

Chapter Objectives

- To understand the principles of displaying XML documents in various formats and devices
- To learn the advantages of separating content from style
- To learn how to write and use Cascading Style Sheets with XML documents
- To evaluate the benefits and drawbacks of Cascading Style Sheets
- To gain an overview of the new Extensible Stylesheet Language for XML

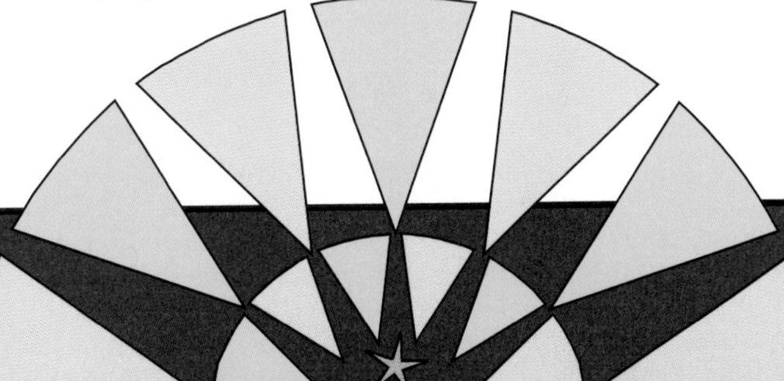

Creating the Presentation

So far, you have learned how to apply syntax rules and how to construct the various pieces of an XML document. Once you have a structured, well-formed document, you will probably want to display the information in some way—in a Web browser, in print, on the display of a handheld computer or Web-enabled phone, as a Portable Document Format (PDF) file, and so on. Using XML to describe your data makes it easy to create multiple presentation layouts for the same data.

This chapter discusses how to use Cascading Style Sheets (CSS). It also briefly covers the new Extensible Stylesheet Language (XSL). Because XSL is new, it is not supported in very many products and programs. "Online References" at the end of the chapter tells you where you can find more information about XSL.

The Benefits of Separating Content from Style

As you have learned, one of the strengths of XML is that it can be used to create languages that describe data, separating the presentation from the style information. Unlike HTML, which defines formatting properties for text but tells you nothing about the data itself, XML elements can be defined according to the nature of the data and can be used for any number of purposes.

Separating the content from the presentation information also allows you to change your presentation layout or method without having to modify the data files, and it allows you to apply one style sheet to any number of documents. For example, a stock brokerage firm that receives stock price data in XML format could develop one style sheet that contains the formatting information for hundreds of stock price XML documents. Or it could create multiple style sheets for presenting this data to customers: one for customers who request stock prices via a Web browser, another one for customers who request stock prices using a wireless Palm Pilot, and yet another for customers who call an automated phone line. The firm could also use the stock price XML files to load a database or send as input to a program.

Using Cascading Style Sheets

CSS was introduced as a recommendation from the W3C in 1996 as CSS1 (Cascading Style Sheets Level 1). CSS2, introduced in 1998, added features and functionality to CSS1. Its primary purpose was to provide HTML authors with more formatting support and to give them a way to apply uniform styles to multiple documents.

CSS style sheets work with XML in the same way that they work with HTML, so if you are familiar with using CSS with HTML documents, it will be an easy transition for you to use it with XML. To use CSS to format XML documents, you need a fairly recent version of a Web browser.

CSS Syntax and Properties

CSS **style sheets** contain rules and declarations that tell a program, such as a Web browser, how to display certain elements. The style information resides in an external file that usually ends with a `.css` file extension. CSS files are plain text files and can be created and edited in any text editor.

> ☆**TIP** Because the CSS1 specification has been around for many years, Web browser support for it is widespread. Netscape Navigator 4.5 and later and Internet Explorer 3.0 and later both support CSS.

You can apply many types of styles to XML documents. The CSS specification is huge, and this chapter covers only a subset of its styles and declarations. For more information and examples, see the sites listed under "Online References" at the end of this chapter.

Style Sheet Declaration

To use a style sheet with your XML document, you must declare its location at the top of the document in the document prolog section. Following is the syntax of the style sheet declaration:

```
<?xml-stylesheet type="text/css" href="styles.css"?>
```

The declaration begins with `<?xml-stylesheet`, followed by the type of style sheet being declared (`text/css`)—in this case, a plain text CSS style sheet—followed by the location of the style sheet file (`styles.css`), and ending with the closing delimiter `?>`. The location of the style sheet can be the local machine or the Internet. To use a style sheet that is located on the Internet, use a URL for the `href` attribute:

Style sheet file located on the Internet

```
<?xml-stylesheet type="text/css"
href="http://www.acme.com/styles.css"?>
```

CSS Rules Syntax

CSS rules have two parts: an element selector, followed by a set of properties declarations separated by semicolons. The element selector can contain a list of elements that all have the same style. The elements in the list are separated by commas. Following are a couple of simple CSS rules:

Rules for a single element: `<address>`

```
address {
    font-size: 12pt;
    font-family: arial
    }
```

The following rules apply to two elements:

Rules for multiple elements: `<address>` and `<city>`

```
address, city {
    font-size: 12pt;
    font-family: arial
    }
```

The two rules—`font-size` and `font-family`—will be applied to the element `<address>` in the first example, and to both the `<address>` and the `<city>` elements in the second example.

☆**TIP** For a rule that assigns only one property, no semicolon is needed:

```
address {
  font-size: 12pt    No semicolon needed
  }
```

CSS Comments

The syntax for comments in CSS is different from the syntax you've seen for XML documents and DTDs. Following is an example of a comment in CSS:

```
/* This is a comment */
```

Comments begin with `/*`, followed by the content of the comment and then `*/`. Comment usage in a CSS file is similar to usage in the other documents you've used. Comments are ignored by the processing program.

CSS Properties

You can define many kinds of CSS properties. Table 4.1 covers five of the major property categories and provides a subset of property rules for each: font properties, text properties, color properties, border properties, and display properties.

☆**WARNING** Style sheets are used to format pages that are displayed on the viewer's computer, but not all computers have the same resources. For example, different computers have different numbers of colors available for display; some have millions of colors available, whereas others have only 256. Also, not all font types are available on all computers. If the viewer's computer does not have a certain resource available, it will pick something else, and that may not produce the formatting output you desire. So be careful when setting your styles. It may be better to be conservative with styles that depend on resources that vary from computer to computer.

Table 4.1 CSS Formatting Properties

Property	Description	Value Examples
Font Properties		
`font`	Global font declaration. Can define all font properties in one property.	`font-family, font-style, font-weight, font-size, font-style`
`font-family`	Font (typeface) for display text.	`arial, courier`
`font-size`	Size of font; can use pixels or percentage.	`small, x-small, medium, large, x-large, #12pt`
`font-style`	Style of font.	`italic, bold, oblique`

Property	Description	Value Examples
***Font Properties** (continued)*		
font-variant	Font rendering.	normal, small-caps
font-weight	Darkness of font; use name or number.	normal, light, bold, bolder, 100, 200, 300, 400, etc.
Text Properties		
word-spacing	Amount of space between words in an element.	normal, *number of pixels*
letter-spacing	Amount of space between letters.	normal, *number of pixels*
text-align	Horizontal alignment of text on page.	right, left, center
vertical-align	Vertical alignment of text on page.	baseline, sub, super, top, text-top, middle, bottom, text-bottom, *percentage*
text-indent	How much first line is indented.	0, *number of pixels, percentage*
text-transform	Change case of text.	uppercase, lowercase, capitalize, none
line-height	Amount of space between lines of text.	normal, *number of pixels*
text-decoration	Special controls of text appearance.	underline, overline, blink, line-through, none
Color Properties		
color	Text color.	red, blue, *color code*
background	Global background declaration. Can define all background properties in one property.	background-color, background-image, background-position, background-repeat, background-attachment
background-color	Color of element's background.	*color name*, transparent
background-image	Image to be used as background.	*URL, name of local file*

(continues)

Table 4.1 CSS Formatting Properties *(continued)*

Property	Description	Value Examples
Color Properties *(continued)*		
`background-attachment`	Scrolling of background image with the element.	`scroll`, `fixed`
`background-position`	Position of element's background.	`top`, `center`, `bottom`, `left`, `right`, *percentage*, *number of pixels*
`background-repeat`	Repeat pattern for background image.	`repeat`, `repeat-x`, `repeat-y`, `no-repeat`
Border Properties		
`border-color`	Color of the border of an element.	`red`, `blue`, color code
`border-width`	Width of the border.	`medium`, `thin`, `thick`, *number of pixels*
`border-style`	Style of border.	`none`, `solid`, `double`
`margin-top`	Width of margin at the top of element.	`0`, *number of pixels*, *percentage*
`margin-bottom`	Width of margin at the bottom of element.	`0`, *number of pixels*, *percentage*
`margin-left`	Width of margin at the left side of element.	`0`, *number of pixels*, *percentage*
`margin-right`	Width of margin at the right side of element.	`0`, *number of pixels*, *percentage*
`padding-top`	Amount of padding at top of element.	`0`, *number of pixels*, *percentage*
`padding-bottom`	Amount of padding at bottom of element.	`0`, *number of pixels*, *percentage*
`padding-left`	Amount of padding at left side of element.	`0`, *number of pixels*, *percentage*
`padding-right`	Amount of padding at right side of element.	`0`, *number of pixels*, *percentage*
`clear`	Whether an element permits other elements on its sides.	`none`, `left`, `right`
`float`	Floating element.	`none`, `left`, `right`

Property	Description	Value Examples
Border Properties *(continued)*		
height	Height of an element.	auto, *number of pixels, percentage*
width	Width of section.	auto, *number of pixels, percentage*
Display Properties		
display	Controls display of element.	block, inline, list-item
white-space	White-space formatting.	normal, pre, nowrap
visibility	Controls visibility of element.	inherit, visible, hidden

Let's start with an example. Following is a well-formed XML document similar to one you saw in Chapter Three. The style sheet declaration has been added, along with a few additional <message> elements:

```
<?xml version="1.0" standalone="yes"?>
<?xml-stylesheet type="text/css" href="emails.css"?>
<emails>
        <!-- Begin Message 1 -->
        <message>
                <to>joe&#64;acmeshipping.com</to>
                <from>brenda&#64;xyzcompany.com</from>
                <date_sent>02/12/01</date_sent>
                <subject>Order 10011</subject>
                <body>
                        Joe,
                        Please let me know if order number
                        10011 has shipped.
                        Thanks,
                        Brenda
                </body>
        </message>
        <!-- End Message 1 -->
        <!-- Begin Message 2 -->
        <message>
                <to>sarah&#64;acmeshipping.com</to>
                <from>sam&#64;xyzcompany.com</from>
                <date_sent>03/05/01</date_sent>
                <subject>Invoice Payment</subject>
                <body>
```

```
                        Sarah,
                        The invoice has been paid.
                        Thanks,
                        Sam
                </body>
        </message>
        <!-- End Message 2 -->
        <!-- Begin Message 3 -->
        <message>
            <to>rick&#64;acmeshipping.com</to>
            <from>john&#64;xyzcompany.com</from>
            <date_sent>01/26/01</date_sent>
            <subject>Meeting</subject>
            <body>
                Rick,
                Please call me about the meeting.
                Thanks,
                John
            </body>
        </message>
        <!-- End Message 3 -->
</emails>
```

Following is the style sheet, emails.css, for this XML document.

```
1 to, from      {
2               font-weight:bold;
3               text-align:left;
4               border-style:solid
5               }
6 date_sent     {
7               font-style:italic;
8               color:blue
9               }
10 subject      {
11              text-decoration:underline;
12              background-color:green;
13              color:yellow
14              }
15 body         {
16              margin-top:10;
17              display:block
18              }
```

Here's a line-by line description:

- Line 1 declares that the properties to follow are rules for both the <to> and the <from> elements.

- Line 2 defines the `font-weight` of the text to be bold for these two elements.
- Line 3 defines the `text-alignment` to be the left side of the screen.
- Line 4 defines the `border-style` of the elements to be solid. This will draw a box around the elements with a solid line.
- Line 5 ends the properties rules for the elements.
- Line 6 declares that the properties to follow are rules for the `<date_sent>` element.
- Line 7 defines the `font-style` to be italic.
- Line 8 defines the `color` of the font as blue.
- Line 9 ends the properties rules for the element.
- Line 10 declares that the properties to follow are rules for the `<subject>` element.
- Line 11 defines the `text-decoration` as an underline. This will underline the text in the content of the element.
- Line 12 defines the `background-color` of the element to be green.
- Line 13 defines the `color` of the font as yellow.
- Line 14 ends the properties rules for the element.
- Line 15 declares that the properties to follow are rules for the `<body>` element.
- Line 16 defines the `margin-top` as 10 points. This property sets the spacing above the element.
- Line 17 defines the `display` as block. The block display results in a carriage return before and after the element, thereby creating line breaks.
- Line 18 ends the properties rules for the element.

Figure 4.1 shows the document in Internet Explorer.

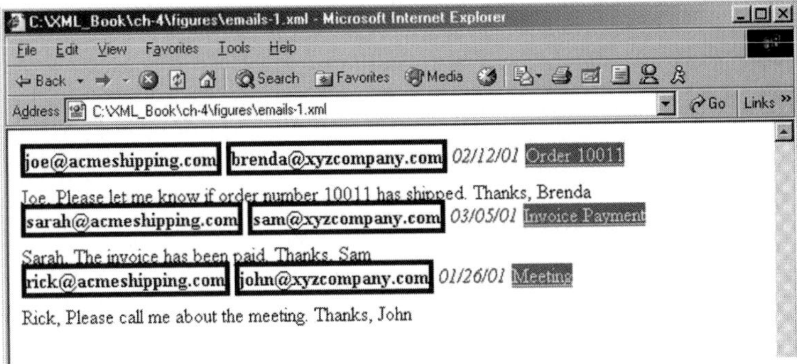

Figure 4.1 XML Document with Style Sheet Applied

☆ **SHORTCUT** To create this example, use a text editor to create two files: the XML file (`emails.xml`) and the CSS style sheet (`emails.css`). Save both files into the same directory on your hard drive. Then open the XML file in Internet Explorer, and you should see the formatted document.

Default Values

If you want to apply default rules to all of the elements in a document unless an element explicitly overrides the rule, you can use the special declaration *:

```
1 message        {
2                display:block;
3                margin-top:50;
4                }
5 to, from       {
6                font-weight:bold;
7                text-align:left;
8                border-style:solid
9                }
10 date_sent     {
11               font-style:italic;
12               color:blue
13               }
14 subject       {
15               text-decoration:underline;
16               background-color:green;
17               color:yellow
18               }
19 body          {
20               margin-top:10;
21               display:block
22               }
23  *            {
24               color:green        Default rule
25               }
```

Adding to the style sheet shown earlier, lines 23–25 declare the default font color to be green. Unless an element overrides this setting, its font color will be green. The elements `<date_sent>` and `<subject>` explicitly define the font color in their own declarations, and that overrides the green font setting from the default element.

Let's apply this style sheet to the XML document shown earlier. Figure 4.2 shows the document in a browser.

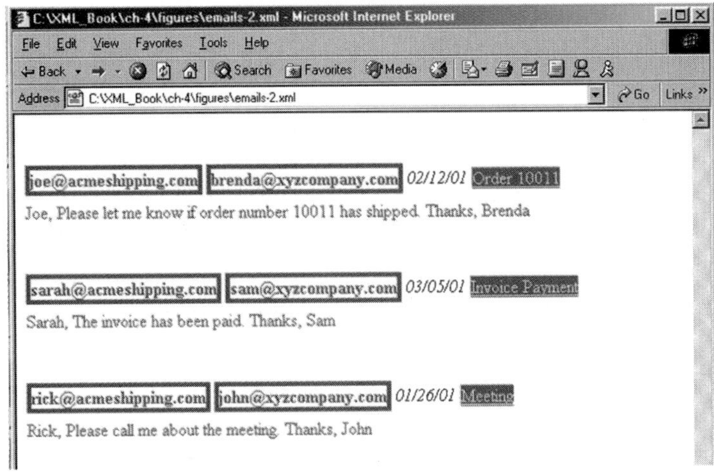

Figure 4.2 XML Document Showing Default Style Value

Property Inheritance

As you have learned, XML documents are composed of many elements with various kinds of relationships to one another. You learned about parent, child, and sibling elements in Chapter Two. This hierarchy of elements is applied to CSS in the form of **property inheritance**: Properties defined for parent elements are passed along to child elements unless the child element overrides them. For example, if the parent of an element sets its font size to 18 points, the child elements will also have a font size of 18 points unless they declare their own rules to override the rules defined by the parent.

Using the sample XML document, let's define a new style sheet:

```
body            {
                display:block;
                color:green;
                font-style:normal;
                font-size:12
                }
from            {
                color:white;
                background-color:green
                }
message         {
                display:block;
                margin-top:50;
                color:blue;
                background-color:yellow;
                font-size:20;
                font-style:italic;
                border-style:double
                }
```

Lines 11–19 are the property rules for the <message> element, which is the parent element. These rules will be applied to all the child elements of <message> unless they are overridden by the child element. Lines 1–6 define property rules for the <body> element, and lines 7–10 define rules for the <from> element that override the rules set in the parent element, <message>. Figure 4.3 shows the XML document in a browser.

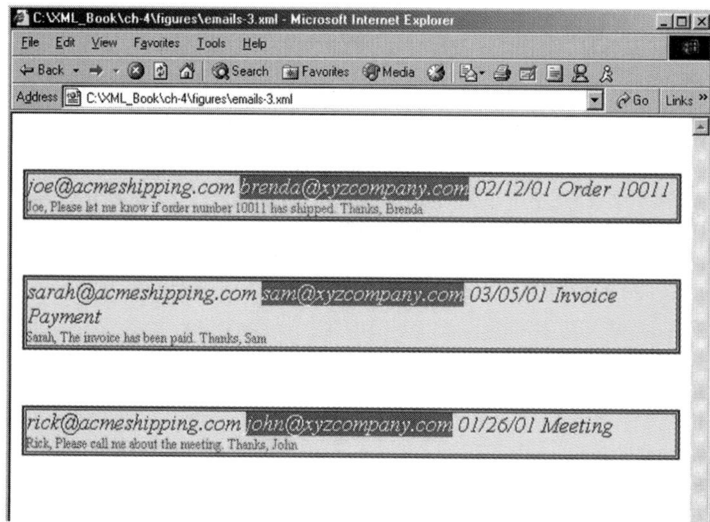

Figure 4.3 XML Document Showing Inheritance

☆ **SHORTCUT** Try the following to apply your style sheet to multiple XML documents:

1. Create a style sheet document, `emails.css`, in a text editor.
2. Instead of using one XML document, create three XML documents in a text editor, one for each message from the XML document shown earlier. Be sure to include the XML and CSS declarations in each of the three files.
3. Save your three XML documents and one CSS file into the same directory on your hard drive.
4. Open each of the XML documents in Internet Explorer.

Notice that all your XML documents use the same style sheet rules and are formatted in the same way.

The Pros and Cons of CSS

CSS has proved to be a wonderful tool for Web developers over the years, giving them much more control over the layout and look of their documents than HTML alone. CSS is simple to learn and provides many powerful formatting styles. One of its biggest advantages in the marketplace is the wide support of its specification in current browsers, and the fact that many Web developers are already familiar with writing CSS style sheets for HTML documents.

However, CSS is not a programming language, and that limits its usefulness in some ways. Here are some of its weaknesses:

- When displayed, elements must appear in the same order in which they appear in an XML document. For example, here is a piece of the sample XML document:

  ```
  <to>joe&#64;acmeshipping.com</to>
  <from>brenda&#64;xyzcompany.com</from>
  <date_sent>02/12/01</date_sent>
  ```

  The order of these elements is `<to>`, `<from>`, `<date_sent>` in the XML document. CSS has no way to rearrange these elements when displaying them in a browser to, for example, show the date first. They will always appear in the same order in which they appear in the XML document.
- It cannot perform mathematical computations and cannot make logical decisions. For example, it cannot display an element in blue if it has one child element, and in orange if it has two child elements.
- Although CSS supports inheritance from parent to child elements, it does not support relationships between and among sibling elements.
- CSS cannot automatically generate text or content. For example, it cannot generate page numbers or header/footer information on pages to be printed.

Overview of XSL

The Extensible Stylesheet Language is a new set of technologies under development by the W3C. XSL addresses the limitations of CSS while also providing an enhanced means of formatting XML documents. W3C released the XSL Recommendation in October 2001. Whereas CSS style sheets are designed to format content for display in a Web browser, XSL style sheets will provide presentation options for a much wider range of output formats, including voice and print.

CSS style sheets apply well to HTML and XML documents, but XSL is being developed specifically for XML documents. XSL comprises two major components: XSL Formatting Objects (XSL-FO), a document formatting vocabulary; and XSL Transformations (XSLT), a language for transforming XML documents from one form to another. The most widely used application of XSLT is to transform XML documents to HTML. Chapter Seven covers some examples of XSL.

XSL provides much greater control and flexibility than CSS because XSL behaves more like a programming language and will have built-in support for functions and templates. One downside, however, is that the current draft specification for XSL is complex, making it much harder to learn and use than CSS.

WARNING XSL is a new specification, and most browsers do not support XSL style sheets as this book is being written. If you are developing style sheets to format XML documents to work in current browsers, CSS is probably the better choice for now.

Summary

- Cascading Style Sheets and the Extensible Stylesheet Language can be used to format XML documents.
- XML separates presentation style from the data of the document, allowing you to create many different styles for one XML document depending on how the document will be used. For example, you can have one style that formats the document for the Internet, and another one that formats it for printing.
- Style sheets contain structure rules that allow you to determine the format and presentation of XML documents. The two primary technologies used for XML style sheets are Cascading Style Sheets (CSS) and Extensible Stylesheet Language (XSL). CSS, the most widely used style sheet technology, was originally developed for use with HTML documents, but it also works well with XML. CSS uses property rules to define various presentation styles and settings, including those for font, text, border, display, and color. CSS properties can be inherited from parent element to child element.
- Although CSS gives XML document authors a great deal of control over document formatting, it is not a programming language and consequently is limited in its scope.
- XSL promises to provide many enhanced features over CSS but is still in development by the W3C.

Online References

W3C CSS Specification
`http://www.w3.org/Style/CSS`

W3C XSL Recommendation
`http://www.w3.org/TR/xsl`

W3C XSL and XSLT Information
`http://www.w3.org/Style/XSL/`

W3C Recommendation for Associating Stylesheets with XML Documents
`http://www.w3.org/TR/xml-stylesheet/`

Webreview Style Sheet Reference Guide and Browser Support
`http://www.webreview.com/style/css1/charts/mastergrid.shtml`

Webmonkey Stylesheet Guide
`http://hotwired.lycos.com/webmonkey/reference/stylesheet_guide/`

CSS Property and Syntax
`http://www.blooberry.com/indexdot/css/`

W3C CSS Validator
`http://jigsaw.w3.org/css-validator/`

☆Review Questions

1. What are a few benefits of separating content from style in an XML document?
2. What are the two types of style sheets that can be used with XML documents?
3. How can CSS style sheets be used to provide style information to many documents?
4. What is a style property, and how is it used to define a particular formatting style for an element?
5. What type of declaration would you use if you wanted all the text to be displayed in the Arial typeface?
6. Define property inheritance, and explain how it can be used to format elements.
7. List two weaknesses of CSS.
8. What are the proposed two primary components of XSL?

☆Hands-On Exercises

1. Write the style sheet declaration statement for a style sheet at the following location:

   `http://www.acmecompany.com/styles.css`
2. Create the property rules for an element called `<title>` that has the following formatting styles: font size of 12 points, bold font, blue text color.
3. Write a style sheet declaration that sets the default text color to red for the entire document.
4. Create a style sheet for the following XML document that will produce the output shown. Do not use default properties; instead, define styles for each element in its own set of properties.

```
<?xml version="1.0" standalone="yes"?>
<?xml-stylesheet type="text/css"
href="exercise-4.css"?>
<business_card>
   <company>Acme Shoe Company</company>
   <address>
      <street>123 High Street</street>
      <city>Boston</city>
```

```
      <state>MA</state>
      <zip>02109</zip>
    </address>
    <phone>617-555-1234</phone>
  </business_card>
```

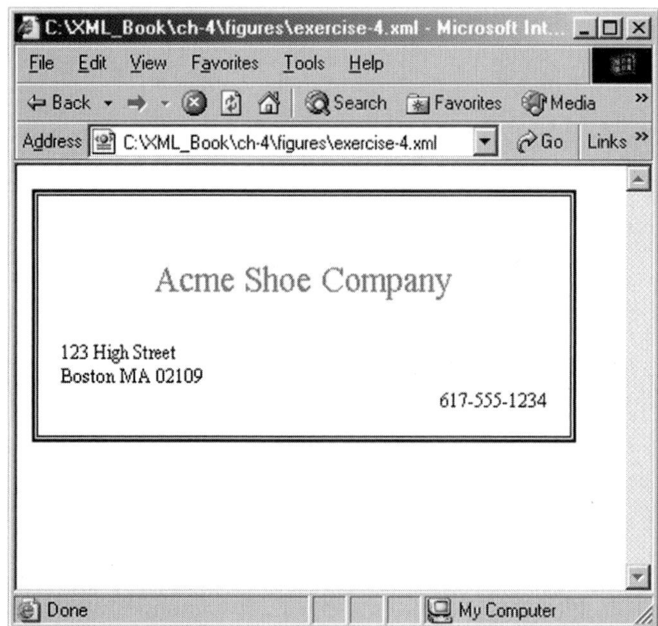

5. Create a style sheet for the same XML document as in Exercise 4, this time using the parent element, <address>, to define the default styles for all its child elements.

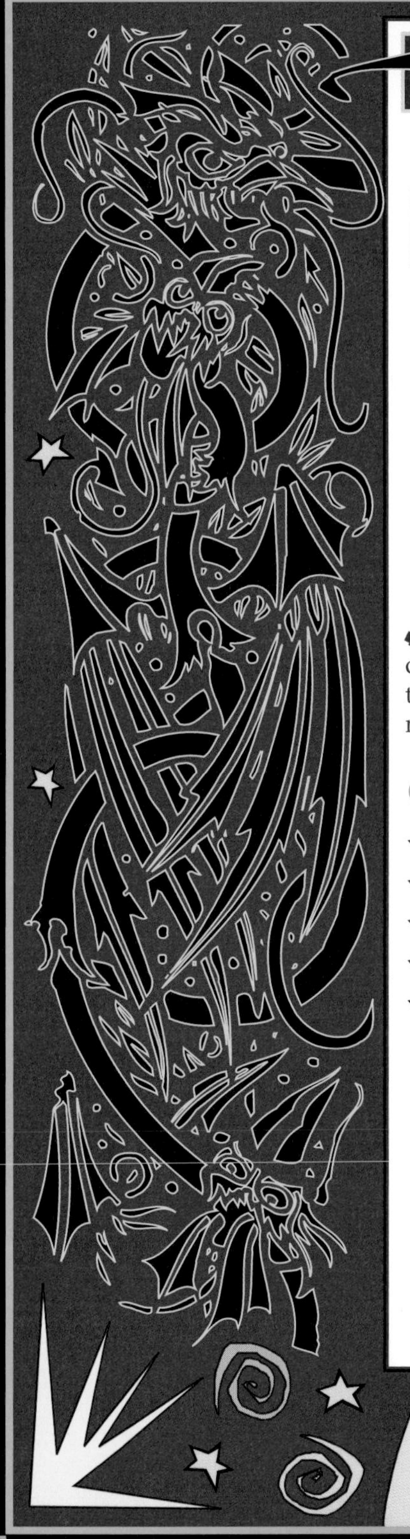

CHAPTER FIVE

NAMESPACES IN XML

Sometimes, elements from different XML documents may have the same name but different meanings within different contexts. These discrepancies can confuse a program that is processing the document. To avoid this confusion, XML uses namespaces to group similar elements.

Chapter Objectives

- To understand what a namespace is
- To define the purpose of namespaces in XML
- To learn how to use namespaces
- To understand the scope of namespace declarations
- To learn how to use namespaces to solve naming collisions in XML documents

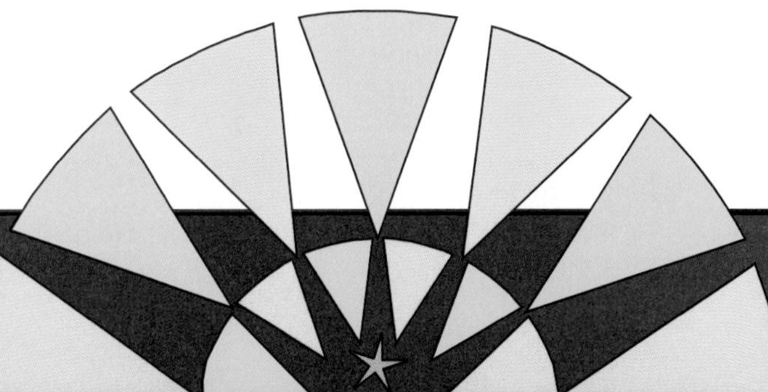

What Is a Namespace?

The XML recommendation from the W3C states that element and attribute names make up the **vocabulary** of a markup language. This concept of vocabulary is similar to that of spoken languages. For example, an English dictionary contains the vocabulary of the English language, and a Spanish dictionary contains the vocabulary of the Spanish language. Certain words with the same spelling may appear in both dictionaries but have completely different meanings depending on which language is being used. For example, the English word *sale* refers to selling something, but the Spanish word *sale* refers to making an exit. The primary purpose of namespaces is to avoid confusion about the meanings of two element names that are spelled the same but have different meanings in the context of different document types.

An XML **namespace** is a group, or set, of element and attribute names that belong to or describe a particular document type. Within a namespace, each of the names must be unique, and the names within the namespace usually have some relation to one another. A namespace is simply a way of assigning certain elements to a particular type within a document.

Let's use a book document type as an example. Here are a few elements that a book document might contain:

- `<title>`
- `<author>`
- `<isbn_number>`
- `<publishing_company>`
- `<date>`
- `<chapter_name>`

All these elements relate to a book. If you were using the book document type within a larger context—for example, a library—you would use a namespace to assign these elements to the namespace for the book element so as not to confuse the `<title>` of a book with the `<title>` of a magazine article.

Why Are Namespaces Needed in XML?

Because XML authors can create their own element names for their markup languages, there is a good chance that multiple authors will use the same element name to describe different topics or concepts. Then when XML documents are merged, the processing program encounters the same name with different meanings. The result is confusion.

Let's look at an example using the element `<bat>` in two document types. Document 1 has to do with baseball equipment:

Why Are Namespaces Needed in XML?

```
<baseball_equipment>
   <ball/>
   <bat/>
   <plate/>
   <helmet/>
</baseball_equipment>
```

Here 'bat' refers to a piece of equipment used in baseball

Document 2 has to do with nocturnal animals:

```
<nocturnal_animals>
   <raccoon/>
   <bat/>
   <owl/>
   <fox/>
</nocturnal_animals>
```

Here 'bat' refers to a flying mammal

The element <bat> is used in both documents but has a different meaning depending on the context in which it is used. Humans can easily distinguish the difference because of the surrounding elements. But an XML processor that needs to merge these two documents would not be able to make this distinction and would treat the two <bat> elements the same. The XML processor is programmed to treat all <bat> elements in a certain way and would not treat the baseball "bat" element any differently from the flying mammal "bat" element.

☆ **TIP** When a single element name has two different meanings within a document, a **naming collision** is said to have occurred.

Using Namespaces to Avoid Confusion

Namespaces are used to avoid the confusion caused by naming collisions. Assigning elements and attributes to namespaces helps to keep them distinct within their own contexts if the document is ever merged with another document that contains some of the same element names.

Let's look at another example. Suppose you are creating a course catalog and you want to include information about the course content and the book used in the course. Here are the two documents. Document 1 contains the course information:

```
<course_information>
   <title>Introduction to XML</title>
   <professor>Jane Smith</professor>
   <meeting_time>Monday, 5:30-7:30</meeting_time>
   <description>This course examines the basics of XML
   </description>
</course_information>
```

Document 2 contains information about the book:

```
<book>
   <title>The Web Wizard's Guide to XML</title>
   <author>C Hughes</author>
   <publishing_company>Addison-Wesley
   </publishing_company>
</book>
```

Here is how these two documents might be merged to create a listing in the catalog document:

```
1  <catalog>
2     <course>
3        <title>Introduction to XML</title>
4        <professor>Jane Smith</professor>
5        <meeting_time>Monday, 5:30-7:30</meeting_time>
6        <description>This course covers the basics of XML...
         </description>
9        <title>The Web Wizard's Guide to XML</title>
10       <author>C Hughes</author>
11       <publishing_company>Addison-Wesley</publishing_company>
14    </course>
15 </catalog>
```

Naming collision

This merged document has two distinct uses of the <title> element. An XML processor would not be able to tell that the first occurrence (on line 3) is being used to list the title of the course, and the second occurrence (on line 9) is being used to list the title of the book. In the following sections, you will learn how to use namespaces to solve this problem.

XML Namespace Syntax

In order to assign certain elements to a particular document type, like baseball equipment, you will need to specify in the XML document which elements belong to this particular type. The next few sections will show you the syntax how to declare a namespace that can be used to assign a type to certain elements, and also how to include elements in this namespace.

The Namespace Declaration

As with other components of XML, namespaces must be declared before they are used. The namespace declaration is placed in the start tag of an element and applies only to that element and its descendants. The namespace declaration looks like an attribute for an element, but it is not, and it should not be treated as such. The scope of namespace declarations follows the same rules as the scope for elements, and namespaces can be nested. (Scope is discussed in detail later in this chapter.)

Namespace declarations fall into two types: default and prefixed.

Default Namespace Declarations

A **default** namespace declaration has the following syntax:

```
xmlns="URI"
```

This declaration consists of the keyword `xmlns`, followed by a Uniform Resource Identifier (URI) enclosed in quotes. The URI is used only as a unique identifier for the namespace. Later in this chapter you will learn about the usage of URIs.

A default namespace declaration on an element applies to that element and all its descendants, unless the descendants have their own namespace declarations. If the root element has a namespace declaration, any elements within the document that do not have an explicit declaration belong to this namespace.

Here are a few examples of default namespace declarations:

```
xmlns="http://chughes.com/XML/namespaces/employee"
xmlns="http://chughes.com/XML/namespaces/company"
xmlns="http://www.w3.org/1999/xhtml"
```

Here is an example of how to use a default namespace declaration in an XML document:

```
1 <meeting xmlns ="http://chughes.com/XML/namespaces/agenda">
2    <topic>First topic on the agenda</topic>
3    <room_number>2117</room_number>
4 </meeting>
```

In this example, the `http://chughes.com/XML/namespaces/agenda` namespace is declared on line 1. Because it is a default namespace, all the elements—`<meeting>`, `<topic>`, and `<room_number>`—belong to this namespace.

Prefixed Namespace Declarations

A **prefixed** namespace declaration has the following syntax:

```
xmlns:prefix="URI"
```

In contrast to the default declaration, with a prefixed namespace an element name must contain the prefix name in its start and end tags in order to belong to the namespace. Here are a few examples of prefixed namespace declarations:

```
xmlns:employee="http://chughes.com/XML/namespaces/employee"
xmlns:company="http://chughes.com/XML/namespaces/company"
xmlns:xlink="http://www.w3.org/1999/xlink"
```

Prefixes for the namespaces

Here is an example of how to use prefixed namespace declarations in an XML document:

```
1 <agenda:meeting xmlns:agenda="http://chughes.com/XML/
  namespaces/agenda">
2    <agenda:topic>First topic on the agenda</agenda:topic>
3    <room_number>2117</room_number>
4 </agenda:meeting>
```

In this example, line 1 declares the prefix for the namespace `http://chughes.com/XML/namespaces/agenda` to be `agenda:`. The elements `<topic>` and `<meeting>` on lines 1 and 2, are in this namespace, as indicated by the use of the prefix `agenda:` before the name of the element in both the start and end tags. The element on line 3, `<room_number>`, does not have the `agenda:` prefix and therefore is not in the namespace.

> ☆**TIP** Elements within a prefixed namespace are called **qualified names**. In the meeting example, the elements `<topic>` and `<meeting>` are qualified names because they are part of the prefixed namespace `http://chughes.com/XML/namespaces/agenda`.

URIs in XML Namespaces

As mentioned previously, a URI is used as a label to uniquely identify the namespace. A URI can take the form of either a URL (Uniform Resource Locator) or URN (Uniform Resource Name), but the URI serves no purpose except as an identifier for a namespace.

> ☆**WARNING** Earlier, a URL was used as the URI to identify the namespaces (`http://chughes.com/XML/namespaces/agenda`). This usage can cause confusion because it looks like a Web address, but it is not. The XML processor will not go to this Web address when it sees it in the namespace declaration and try to validate the namespace against a document that resides at that address. In fact, in most cases, this URL is a fictitious address, and there is no document at the Web address referenced by the URL. The URL serves only as a unique identifying label for the namespace.

The main reason that URLs are used as URIs for namespaces is that URLs are unique. Most authors of XML documents, whether individuals or companies, own a domain name to which they have exclusive rights; this means that they can guarantee that their namespace identifiers will be unique by constructing fictitious URLs based on their domain names. The URIs must be unique to ensure that no two declarations have the same URI.

For example, the domain name `chughes.com` is a unique domain name. The following namespace declarations could be used to uniquely identify different namespaces:

```
xmlns:book="http://chughes.com/XML/namespaces/book"
xmlns:jazz="http://chughes.com/XML/namespaces/music/jazz"
xmlns="http://chughes.com/XML/namespaces/employee"
xmlns="http://chughes.com/XML/namespaces/company"
```

Lines 1 and 2 declare prefixed namespaces, and lines 3 and 4 are default declarations. All use URLs as the URI identifier for the namespaces.

The second type of URI that can be used is a URN. The syntax for URNs is defined by the IETF (Internet Engineering Task Force). The IETF is an organization that defines standards for the Internet. (For more information, see "Online References" at the end of the chapter.) The syntax is as follows:

```
1 xmlns="urn:namespace_identifier:namespace_string"
2 xmlns:prefix="urn:namespace_identifier:namespace_string"
```

Line 1 is the syntax for a default namespace declaration, and line 2 is the syntax for a prefixed declaration. The `namespace identifier` and `namespace string` are two pieces of information that are used to uniquely identify the namespace in a URN.

Following are examples of URNs:

```
1 xmlns:jazz="urn:chughes.com:music-jazz"
2 xmlns="urn:chughes.com:employee"
3 xmlns="urn:loc.gov:book"
4 xmlns:isbn="urn:ISBN:0-395-36341-6"
```

Lines 1 and 4 declare prefixed namespaces, and lines 2 and 3 are default declarations. Lines 3 and 4 are examples from the W3C's namespace recommendation.

> ☆ **SHORTCUT** If you use namespaces, you may want to purchase a domain name so that your namespaces will be unique. This will ensure that no one else will use your URIs.

URIs can be confusing, but remember, the purpose of a URI is simply to provide a unique identity for the namespace. URIs that contain URLs are not providing a Web address that contains data about the namespace at that location, and an XML application will not try to visit that Web address when it sees it in a namespace declaration.

How to Determine the Scope of a Namespace

The **scope** of a namespace determines which elements can belong to a namespace within a document. This can get tricky, especially if you are using a combination of default and prefixed namespaces in the same document. The scope of a namespace depends on the hierarchy of elements in the document.

The scope of a particular namespace cannot ascend above the element on which it is declared in the hierarchy of elements. Namespaces can only descend an element hierarchy. For example, a namespace that is declared on an element can be applied to any of its child elements, but a namespace declared on a child element cannot be applied to that element's parent element or to sibling elements. Let's look at a few examples.

Here is an example of a company newsletter document without any namespace declarations. You will use this document in the examples that follow.

```
1  <newsletter>
2     <name>ACME Company Newsletter</name>
3     <article>
4        <title>Company Employees Participate in 5K Run</title>
5        <author>J. Fraser</author>
6     </article>
7     <issue>July, 2001</issue>
8  </newsletter>
```

Example 1: Declaring a Default Namespace

If you assign a default namespace to the root element, <newsletter>, that namespace will apply to all the other elements in this document because they are all descendants of <newsletter> and no additional namespaces are defined.

```
1  <newsletter xmlns="http://chughes.com/firstnamespace">
2     <name>ACME Company Newsletter</name>
3     <article>
4        <title>Company Employees Participate in 5K Run</title>
5        <author>J. Fraser</author>
6     </article>
7     <issue>July, 2001</issue>
8  </newsletter>
```

In this example, all the elements—<newsletter>, <name>, <article>, <title>, <author>, and <issue>—are in the http://chughes.com/firstnamespace namespace because the namespace was declared on the <newsletter> element, which is the parent element of all the other elements in the document.

Example 2: Declaring Two Default Namespaces

You can add a second default namespace declaration to the <article> element on line 3 that applies only to the <article> element and its child elements: <title> and <author>.

```
1  <newsletter xmlns="http://chughes.com/firstnamespace">
2     <name>ACME Company Newsletter</name>
3     <article xmlns="http://chughes.com/secondnamespace">
4        <title>Company Employees Participate in 5K Run</title>
5        <author>J. Fraser</author>
6     </article>
7     <issue>July, 2001</issue>
8  </newsletter>
```

Elements within the http://chughes.com/secondnamespace namespace

The two child elements of <article> (<title> and <author> on lines 4 and 5) are within the scope of the first default namespace, http://chughes.com/firstnamespace, declared on the <newsletter> element on line 1; but the second namespace, http://chughes.com/

How to Determine the Scope of a Namespace

secondnamespace, assigned on the <article> element on line 3, takes precedence because it is the closest to these elements in the hierarchy.

The <issue> element is in the first default namespace because it is outside the closing tag for the <article> element, meaning that it is out of the scope of the second namespace; but it is still within the scope of the first namespace because the <issue> element is a child element of <newsletter>.

Example 3: Declaring a Default and a Prefixed Namespace

Now let's change the second namespace declaration to a prefixed declaration.

```
1  <newsletter xmlns="http://chughes.com/firstnamespace">
2     <name>ACME Company Newsletter</name>
3     <flag:article xmlns:flag="http://chughes.com/
      secondnamespace">
4        <flag:title>Company Employees Participate in 5K Run
         </flag:title>
5        <author>J. Frasier</author>
6     </flag:article>
7     <issue>July, 2001</issue>
8  </newsletter>
```

Elements within the http://chughes.com/secondnamespace namespace

Notice that the prefix flag is now associated with the second namespace on line 3, http://chughes.com/secondnamespace, and can apply only to elements within the scope of the <article> element. Both the <article> and the <title> elements contain the prefix, so in this example, both are part of the second namespace. The <author> element does not contain the prefix and is therefore not in the second namespace. However, it is still within the scope of the first namespace, so it belongs to the http://chughes.com/firstnamespace namespace that is declared on the <newsletter> element in line 1. All the other elements in this document that do not have the flag prefix are part of the first namespace, http://chughes.com/firstnamespace.

Example 4: Out-of-Scope Example

Here, you add the prefix for the second namespace, flag, to the <issue> element on line 7 to demonstrate the concept of being out of scope.

```
1  <newsletter xmlns="http://chughes.com/firstnamespace">
2     <name>ACME Company Newsletter</name>
3     <flag:article xmlns:flag="http://chughes.com/
      secondnamespace">
4        <flag:title>Company Employees Participate in 5K Run
         </flag:title>
5        <author>J. Frasier</author>
6     </flag:article>
7     <flag:issue>July, 2001</flag:issue>
8  </newsletter>
```

Out of scope for the http://chughes.com/secondnamespace namespace

☆ **WARNING** Namespaces are not widely supported by browsers. Internet Explorer 5.5 and later has limited support for namespaces.

The <issue> element is not part of the second namespace because the <issue> element is not a child element of the <article> element, meaning that it is outside the scope allowed for this namespace. Because a namespace must be declared before it is used, Internet Explorer displays an error message when this document is viewed, as shown in Figure 5.1.

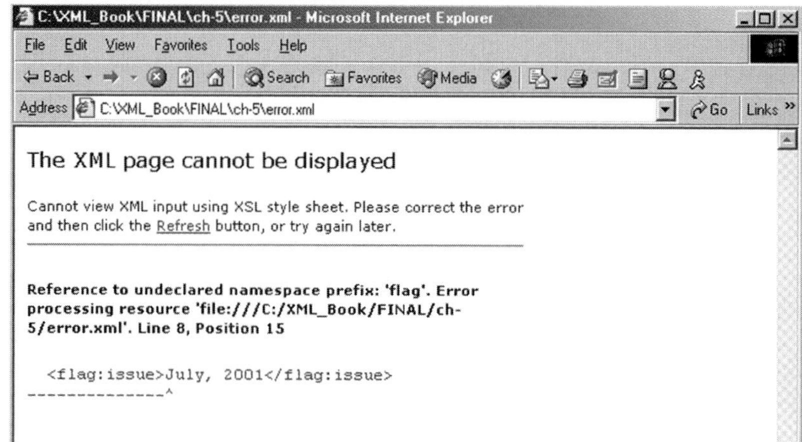

Figure 5.1 Internet Explorer Namespace Declaration Error

To correct this error, one solution is to declare a new namespace on the <issue> element. Because the second namespace declaration ends with the <article> tag, it is legal to use this prefix, flag , again with the third namespace declaration.

```
1  <newsletter xmlns="http://chughes.com/firstnamespace">
2     <name>ACME Company Newsletter</name>
3     <flag:article xmlns:flag="http://chughes.com/
      secondnamespace">
4        <flag:title>Company Employees Participate in 5K Run
         </flag:title>
5        <author>J. Frasier</author>
6     </flag:article>
7     <flag:issue xmlns:flag="http://chughes.com/thirdnamespace">
      July, 2001</flag:issue>
8  </newsletter>
```

Elements within the http://chughes.com/secondnamespace namespace

Element within the http://chughes.com/thirdnamespace namespace

In this example, the first namespace contains the elements <newsletter>, <name>, and <author> on lines 1, 2, and 5. The second namespace contains the <article> and <title> elements on lines 3 and 4. The third namespace contains the <issue> element on line 7.

Using Namespaces in XML Documents

Now that you've learned how to declare a namespace on an element and understand the scope of namespaces within a document, let's use namespaces to correct the naming collision from earlier in the chapter. Here is the document again:

```
<?xml#version="1.0"?>
<catalog>
   <course>
      <title>Introduction to XML</title>
      <professor>Jane Smith</professor>
      <meeting_time>Monday, 5:30-7:30</meeting_time>
      <description>This course covers the basics of XML...
      </description>
      <title>The Web Wizard's Guide to XML</title>
      <author>C Hughes</author>
      <publishing_company>Addison-Wesley</publishing_company>
   </course>
</catalog>
```

☆ **WARNING** There are many ways to solve this problem, and these are not the only ones. The best solution will depend on how the document is used by a program.

Solution 1

Here, you define a default namespace on the <catalog> element and a prefixed namespace on the <course> element. Define a default namespace for the root element, <catalog>, on line 2. This declaration includes all descendant elements of <catalog> that are not specifically assigned to a different namespace. Then you define a prefixed namespace for the <course> element that can be used to differentiate the elements related to the book from the elements about the course.

```
1  <?xml#version="1.0"?>
2  <catalog xmlns="http://chughes.com/XML/namespaces/
   catalog_listings">
3     <course xmlns:book="http://chughes.com/XML/namespaces/book">
4        <title>Introduction to XML</title>
5        <professor>Jane Smith</professor>
6        <meeting_time>Monday, 5:30-7:30</meeting_time>
7        <description>This course covers the basics of XML...
         </description>
8        <book:title>The Web Wizard's Guide to XML</book:title>
9        <book:author>C Hughes</book:author>
10       <book:publishing_company>Addison-Wesley
         </book:publishing_company>
11    </course>
12 </catalog>
```

Elements that belong to the `http://chughes.com/XML/namespaces/book` namespace

In this example, the elements <title>, <author>, and <publishing_company> belong to the http://chughes.com/XML/namespaces/book namespace that is declared on line 3. All the other elements—<catalog>, <course>, <title>, <professor>, <meeting_time>, and <description>—belong to the default namespace, http://chughes.com/XML/namespaces/catalog_listings, which is declared on line 2.

Solution 2

In this solution, you define two different prefixed namespaces for the <course> element to differentiate it from the book information.

```
1   <?xml#version="1.0"?>
2   <catalog>
3      <course xmlns:book="http://chughes.com/XML/namespaces/book"
       xmlns:crse="http://chughes.com/XML/namespaces/
       course_information">
4         <crse:title>Introduction to XML</crse:title>
5         <crse:professor>Jane Smith</crse:professor>
6         <crse:meeting_time>Monday, 5:30-7:30</crse:meeting_time>
7         <crse:description>This course covers the basics of XML...
          </description>
```

Elements that belong to the http://chughes.com/XML/namespaces/course_information namespace

```
8         <book:title>The Web Wizard's Guide to XML</book:title>
9         <book:author>C Hughes</book:author>
10        <book:publishing_company>Addison-Wesley
          </book:publishing_company>
11     </crse:course>
12  </catalog>
```

Elements that belong to the http://chughes.com/XML/namespaces/book namespace

The two namespace declarations are defined on line 3 for the <course> element. The elements <title>, <professor>, <meeting_time>, and <description>, on lines 4–7, belong to the http://chughes.com/XML/namespaces/course_information namespace. The elements <title>, <author>, and <publishing_company>, on lines 8–10, belong to the **http://chughes.com/XML/namespaces/book** namespace. The <catalog> and <course> elements on lines 2 and 3 do not belong to any namespace.

☆ **SHORTCUT** If your XML documents will be merged with other documents, it may be a good idea to assign namespaces to your elements to avoid confusion. Even if there are no current conflicts, another XML author could add or change element names and create a conflict in the future.

Summary

- Namespaces define the elements within a markup language's vocabulary.
- A naming collision occurs when an element name has two distinct meanings within the same document. Namespaces help an XML processor to reconcile naming collisions.
- All namespaces must be declared on an element before they are used. Namespace declarations can be of two types: default and prefixed.
- The scope of a namespace declaration within a document depends on the element hierarchy. Namespaces can be applied only to descendants of the element on which the namespace is declared. If a namespace is assigned to an element that is not a descendant of the element that namespace was declared on, the declaration is said to be "out of scope" and will produce an error.
- A URI is a unique identifier for a namespace and can be either a URL or URN. Namespace declarations can be nested within a document.

Online References

W3C Namespaces in XML Recommendation
`http://www.w3.org/TR/REC-xml-names`

Namespace Tutorial-XML.com
`http://www.xml.com/pub/r/672`

Namespaces in XML: Best Practices, Risky Business–XML.com
`http://www.xml.com/pub/r/848`

XML Namespaces by Example
`http://www.xml.com/pub/a/1999/01/namespaces.html`

IETF URN Syntax Memo
`http://www.ietf.org/rfc/rfc2141.txt`

The MathML Namespace
`http://www.w3.org/Math/MathMLNamespace.html`

W3C XHTML Recommendation 1.0
`http://www.w3.org/TR/xhtml`

W3C Naming and Addressing: URIs, URLs, ...
`http://www.w3.org/Addressing`

Namespaces in XML–XML Cover Pages
`http://xml.coverpages.org/namespaces.html`

☆Review Questions

1. What is the purpose of namespaces in XML?
2. Define a naming collision. When does a naming collision occur?
3. Describe two ways to correct a naming collision.
4. What is the difference in syntax between a default and a prefixed namespace declaration?
5. Name the two types of URIs used to identify namespaces.
6. What does "out of scope" mean, and when does it occur?
7. Can default and prefixed namespaces be used within the same document?
8. Can namespace declarations be applied to the child elements of the element on which the namespace was declared? That element's parent element? That element's sibling elements?
9. Does the element on which the namespace is declared have to belong to the namespace? Can it belong to a different namespace or to no namespace at all?

☆Hands-On Exercises

1. Merge the following two documents into one document. Do not change any of the element names. You will use your new document in Exercises 2 and 3.

   Document 1:

```
<company_info>
  <name>XYZ Beverage Company</name>
  <street>123 Main Street</street>
  <city>Irving</city>
  <state>Texas</state>
  <zip>75063</zip>
</company_info>
```

   Document 2:

```
<company_officers>
  <name>M.B. DeYoung</name>
  <title>Chief Executive Officer</title>
  <name>Susan Silva</name>
  <title>Chief Operating Officer</title>
</company_officers>
```

2. Using the document you created in Exercise 1, use default namespaces to correct the naming conflict caused by the two distinct meanings of the <name> element.
3. Using the document you created in Exercise 1, use prefixed namespaces to correct the naming conflict caused by the two distinct meanings of the <name> element.

4. Convert the following three URNs to URLs using the URL syntax discussed in the chapter:

```
xmlns="urn:schemas-microsoft-com:xml-data"
xmlns:perl="urn:languages-chughes-com:perl"
xmlns="urn:chughes-com:music-country"
```

5. Correct the "out of scope" errors in the following document for the prefixed namespace:

```
<inventory>
  <item>
     <comp:name xmlns:comp="http://chughes.com/XML/
     computer">
     Pentium 700 Computer with 17 Inch Monitor
     </comp:name>
     <comp:quantity>100</comp:quantity>
     <comp:location>Warehouse</comp:location>
  <item>
  <item>
     <comp:name>8 Port Network Hub</comp:name>
     <comp:quantity>35</comp:quantity>
     <comp:location>Shipping Dock</comp:location>
  </item>
</inventory>
```

CHAPTER SIX

LINKS IN XML

One of the technologies that has made the HTML Web a huge success over the past decade is the hyperlink. Hyperlinks make the Web interactive, allowing users to jump from Web page to Web page simply by clicking on these links. XML provides extensive linking functionality that can be used with a number of different programs in addition to the Web.

Chapter Objectives

- To understand what a hyperlink is
- To gain a brief overview of Web hyperlinks in HTML and to understand the differences between XML and HTML links
- To become familiar with the highlights of the W3C specification for XLinks
- To learn the syntax and usage of simple XLinks
- To learn the syntax and usage of extended XLinks

What Is a Link?

A **hyperlink** (also called simply a **link**) is an object in a Web page that visitors can click on to redirect the browser to another Web page or a file. Usually, a hyperlink appears on-screen as blue, underlined text or as an image. Special linking elements are included in the HTML language specification that allow Web page authors to use images or text within a Web page to create these links. The item at the other end of the hyperlink is called the **target resource**. In addition to other Web pages, the target resource can be an image file, a multimedia file (such as an audio or video file), another section within the same page, or any Web page or file anywhere on the Internet. Links provide a powerful means of organizing information and allow Web page authors to create complex, cross-referenced Web sites with clickable menus and tables of contents.

The XML specification for document linking is XLink (XML Linking Language). Because of the huge success of hyperlinks in HTML, the developers of XLink decided to keep the specification as close to the HTML syntax as possible while adding some enhancements.

Overview of Links in HTML

Because XML derives much of its link specification from HTML, let's start with a few examples of how HTML links work. HTML provides a few elements for linking files and documents; we will look at the `<a>` and `<img>` elements.

The <a> Anchor Element

The `<a>`, or **anchor**, element in HTML is used to create hyperlinks. These types of links require the user to perform an action—usually clicking on the link—for the link to do anything. The clickable region of the link can consist of text or images. If the user never clicks the linked image or text, the link is never activated. Following is the syntax of an anchor element in HTML:

```
<a href="http://chughes.com/newpage.html">
This is a link</a>
```

The text "This is a link" would be the clickable area of this link in a Web browser. Figure 6.1 shows what this piece of code looks like in a browser window. The value of the `href` attribute is the URL of the file being linked to, or the target resource.

Let's look at how the anchor element is used. Here is an HTML page that contains a number of links. Figure 6.2 shows the Web page in Internet Explorer.

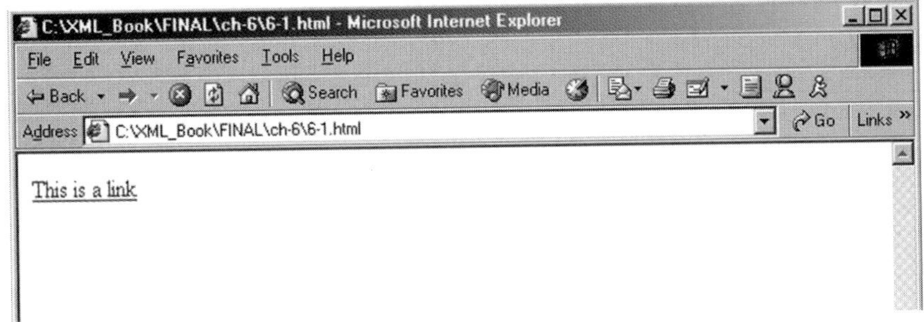

Figure 6.1 A Link in Internet Explorer

```
<html>
   <head>
      <title>Link Examples in HTML</title>
   </head>
   <body>
      <p>    Here are some examples of links in HTML:</p>
      <p>
         <a href="http://chughes.com/newpage.html">
         This is an absolute link to a new page</a>
      </p>
      <p>
         <a href="newpage.html">This is a relative link to a
         new page</a>
      </p>
      <p>
         <a href="newpage.html"><img src="button.gif"
         alt="This image is a clickable button"></a>
      </p>
      <p>
         <a href="mailto:cheryl@chughes.com">This is a link
         that launches an e-mail message</a>
      </p>
    </body>
</html>
```

Hyperlinks in HTML

Overview of Links in HTML

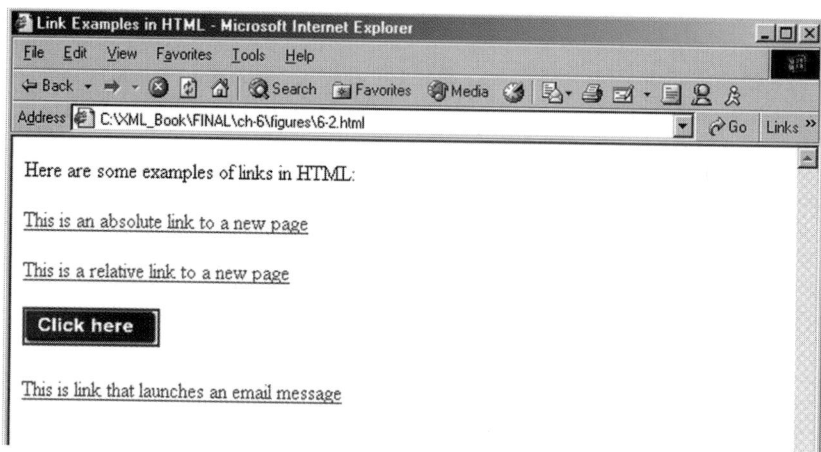

Figure 6.2 HTML Viewed in Internet Explorer

The four links in this file are on lines 8, 11, 14, and 17. Following is a line-by-line explanation of the HTML code for the links:

- The link in line 8 uses an **absolute** URL (`http://chughes.com/newpage.html`), meaning that the entire URL—including the protocol (`http://`) and domain name (`chughes.com`)—has been included in the value of the `href` attribute.
- The link in line 11 uses a **relative** URL (`newpage.html`), meaning that the protocol and domain name pieces have been omitted from the value of the `href` attribute.

TIP Absolute versus Relative URLs in Links

An **absolute URL** is used to link documents that reside on different Web servers. When you use an absolute URL, you include the protocol (`http://`) and domain names (`chughes.com`) to direct the Web browser to the location of the new Web server. This kind of link does not take into account any location information about the current document and can reference any target resource anywhere on the Internet

Examples are `http://chughes.com/newpage.html`, `http://chughes.com/documents/newpage.html`, and `http://chughes.com/images/mypicture.gif`.

A **relative URL** is used to link documents that reside on the same Web server. When you use a relative URL, you omit the protocol and domain name. The link to the target resource is relative to the location of the document containing the link, known as the **source document**. If the target resource resides in the same directory as the source document, you can use a link containing only the name of the target resource, as in the first example shown next. If the target resource resides in a different directory on the Web server, you must include the subdirectory information in the link, as in the other two examples.

Examples are `newpage.html`, `documents/newpage.html`, and `images/mypicture.gif`.

- The link in line 14 is also a relative link, but this link uses an image as the clickable portion. The links in lines 8, 11, and 17 all use text as the clickable portion.
- The link in line 17 launches the default e-mail program and creates a blank e-mail message addressed to the e-mail address referenced in the value of the `href` attribute. The special prefix `mailto:` keyword tells the Web browser that this link should create an e-mail message. Clicking it will launch the visitor's default e-mail program so that she can create a new e-mail message to the recipient address listed in the link (`cheryl@chughes.com`).

The `<img>` Image Element

Many HTML programmers do not think of the `<img>` element as a "linking" element, but it is a type of link that is used to embed images into an HTML page. The `<img>` element, unlike the anchor element discussed in the preceding section, does not require any user intervention, such as clicking on highlighted text, in order to activate the link. Following is the syntax of an `<img>` element:

```
<img src="button.gif" alt="This is a button">
```

> **WARNING** The `<img>` element is an empty element. The syntax of the `<img>` element may look wrong to you based on the rules you have learned about XML. In HTML, however, empty elements need not end in `/>` as in XML. So this syntax is correct for HTML but would be incorrect for XML.

The value of the `src` ("source") attribute, like that of the `href` attribute, is the URL of the target resource—in this case, the image file. The value can be an absolute or relative URL; in this example, it is relative. The value of the `alt` ("alternate") attribute is a text string that will show up in place of the image file if the client application cannot display images. This would be the case for text-based Web browsers, such as the Lynx browser, or for mobile devices such as cell phones or PDAs (personal digital assistants) that cannot display graphics files.

When a Web browser that is parsing an HTML page encounters an `<img>` element, it automatically sends an additional request to the Web server asking for the image file referenced in the `src` attribute. After the image file is returned to the Web browser, it displays the image file in the page at the exact location where the `<img>` element is located in the HTML document. These images are called **inline** images because they are loaded into the browser at the same time as the rest of the HTML document. The link on line 14 in the earlier example uses an image as the clickable piece of the anchor element. Notice in Figure 6.2 that the image of the button shows up automatically when the page is loaded.

Limitations of Linking in HTML

The ability to link documents has been one of the most powerful and popular features of the HTML language. However, HTML links are simple and have many limitations. Following are a few of the shortcomings:

- A link in HTML can point only to one resource as the value of the `href` attribute.

- Links in HTML are **unidirectional**, meaning that after the link is followed, there is no path back to the original document.
- Only certain elements in HTML, such as the `<a>` and `<img>` elements, can be used for linking.

Links in XML

The XLink specification for XML was released as a W3C recommendation in July 2001. Because of the success of HTML linking , the W3C made the XML specification as similar as possible to HTML, with some enhancements. Following are a few of the highlights of the XML XLink specification:

- It supports **multidirectional** links. This allows target resources to link back to the source document or documents.
- Links can contain more than one destination. This allows a single link to point to any number of target resources.
- XML does not confine linking capabilities to a subset of elements. Any XML element can be a linking element.
- The behavior of a link can be defined by the XML programmer.

The XLink specification contains two types of links: simple links and extended links. This chapter discusses the syntax and usage of simple links in detail and reviews examples of how to use them. Extended links are not yet supported by Web browsers, however, so we will briefly review the differences between simple and extended links and look at an example of the extended link syntax, but you won't be able to see it in action.

> ☆**WARNING** XLink's primary drawback is that, because it is so new, it has very little vendor support. The only browser that currently supports simple XLink links is Netscape 6, the browser used for the examples in this chapter. For a browser compatibility chart, see "Online References" at the end of this chapter.

Simple Links

The syntax and functionality of simple links in XML are very similar to those of the `<a>` and `<img>` anchor elements in HTML. **Simple links** are unidirectional and can contain only one link to one target resource. However, they can be defined on any XML element.

All links, both simple and extended, must be defined within the XLink namespace: `http://www.w3c.org/1999/xlink`. To be valid, simple links require two pieces of information: a `type` attribute and an `href` attribute. You will learn more about attributes in the next section. Here is an XML document with a simple link for an element called `<map>`. Figure 6.3 shows what this document looks like in Netscape 6.

```
1  <?xml version="1.0"?>
2  <map
3     xmlns:xlink="http://www.w3.org/1999/xlink"
4     xlink:type="simple"
5     xlink:href="mapimage.gif">
6     Link to Map image
7  </map>
```

Following is an explanation of each line of this example:

- Line 1 is the XML declaration.
- Line 2 begins the <map> element.
- Line 3 defines the namespace to be `http://www.w3.org/1999/xlink` and defines the prefix for the namespace to be `xlink`.
- Line 4 defines the `xlink:type` attribute to be `simple`.
- Line 5 defines the `xlink:href` attribute for the link that contains the URL of the target resource, `mapimage.gif`.
- Line 6 specifies the text for the link, which will be clickable in a browser window.
- Line 7 contains the ending tag for the <map> linking element.

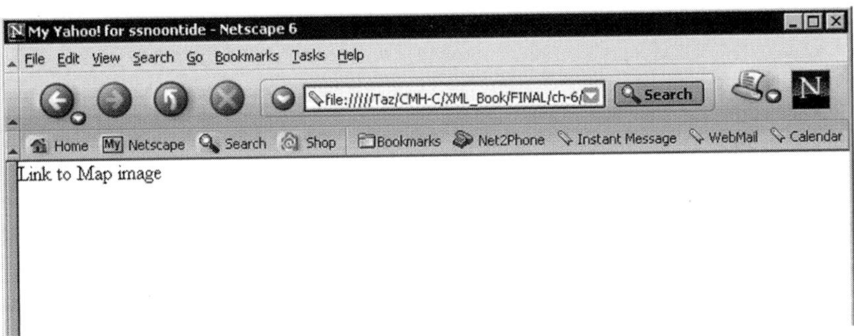

Figure 6.3 XLink Example in Netscape 6

WARNING Notice that the link in Figure 6.3 does not have the appearance of the links in the HTML examples from earlier in the chapter in Figures 6.1 and 6.2. The links in HTML are colored blue and underlined because the browsers are programmed to display links in this way. As you have learned, browsers do not have any "built-in" rules about how to format XML elements, therefore the link in Figure 6.3 does not contain any coloring or underline. If you wanted to add formatting for this link, you would have to create a style sheet to create the formatting properties you want, like the blue font color and underlined text. You learned about CSS style sheets in Chapter Five, and you will learn more about XSL style sheets in Chapter Seven.

☆ SHORTCUT Try this example by following these steps:

1. Create the XML <map> document in a text editor, and save it on your hard drive.
2. Download or create an image called `mapimage.gif`, and save it into the same directory on your hard drive.
3. Open the XML document in Netscape 6 and click on the link.

The page will be replaced with the image file referenced on line 5.

Simple Link Attributes

Table 6.1 defines the attributes that can be used with a simple XLink element. The remainder of this section further describes these attributes and the values that can be used with them.

Table 6.1 Attributes of a Simple XLink

Attribute Name	Required	Description
`type`	Yes	Determines type of link. Value of `simple` is always defined for simple links.
`href`	Yes	Defines the URL of the resource being linked to. Can be either an absolute or a relative link.
`show`	No	Defines the behavior of the link after it is activated. Values can be `replace`, `new embed`, `other`, or `none`.
`actuate`	No	Defines when the link will be activated. Values can be `onRequest`, `onLoad`, `other`, or `none`.
`role`	No	Describes the resource being linked to.
`title`	No	Like a comment, this attribute can be used by the author to describe the link.
`arcrole`	No	Describes the relationship between the source document and the target resource.

The `type` and `href` Attributes

The `type` and `href` attributes are required by a simple XLink. For a simple link, the `type` attribute is always set to the keyword `simple`. The `href` attribute has the same function in XLink as it does in an HTML <a> element: It defines a URL to the link's target resource and can be either an absolute or a relative URL.

The `show` and `actuate` Attributes

The `show` and `actuate` attributes are optional attributes in an XLink element. They let you control how the link behaves. The `show` attribute defines the behavior of the link after it is activated. Following is a brief description of each of the possible values for the `show` attribute:

- `replace`: After a link is activated, the content that resides at the value of the `href` attribute will replace the current content. In other words, the content of the resource being linked to will replace the current document in the window.
- `new`: After a link is activated, the content in the current window will not change. Instead, a new window will be opened that displays the content of the resource being linked to. The end result will be two separate windows: the original window with the content of the source page, and a new window with the content of the target page.
- `embed`: After a link is activated, the content of the resource being linked to should be inserted into the current document at the place where the link exists.
- `other` and `none`: These two attributes are not defined by the XLink specification. Programs can use these two attributes for any purpose.

The `actuate` attribute also defines the behavior of an XLink. This attribute defines when a link will be activated. Following is a brief description of each of the possible values:

- `onRequest`: This value means that the link must be activated manually. This action could be a user clicking on the link content, an action that occurs as the result of a function within a program, or the expiration of a time limit. Works like the `<a>` element in HTML.
- `onLoad`: This value means that the link will automatically be activated at the time the current page is loaded into the window. No other intervention is needed to activate this link. Works like the `<img>` element in HTML.
- `other` and `none`: These two attributes are not defined by the XLink specification. Programs can use these two attributes for any purpose.

The `role`, `arcrole`, and `title` Attributes

The `role`, `arcrole`, and `title` attributes, also optional attributes, are used to describe the link. The `role` attribute is used to describe the resource being linked to, and the `title` attribute is used to describe the link itself. The `role` attribute may also be used by programs to define a link's role within some context of the program. The `arcrole` attribute is similar to the `role` attribute but describes the relationship between the source and target resources.

The following example extends the earlier `<map>` example with several additional attributes. The attributes do not change the way the link is displayed in a browser, so this document would appear the same in the Netscape 6 browser as shown in Figure 6.3.

```
1  <?xml version="1.0"?>
2  <map
3     xmlns:xlink="http://www.w3.org/1999/xlink"
4     xlink:type="simple"
5     xlink:href="mapimage.gif"
6     xlink:actuate="onRequest"
7     xlink:show="replace"
8     xlink:role="image"
9     xlink:title="A map image">
10    Link to Map image
11 </map>
```

Following is an explanation of each line of this example:

- Line 1 is the XML declaration.
- Line 2 begins the <map> element.
- Line 3 defines the namespace to be `http://www.w3.org/1999/xlink` and the prefix for the namespace to be `xlink`.
- Line 4 defines the `xlink:type` attribute to be simple.
- Line 5 defines the `xlink:href` attribute for the link that contains the URL of the target resource, `mapimage.gif`.
- Line 6 defines the `xlink:actuate` attribute to be `onRequest`, which means that the user must click on the link to activate it.
- Line 7 defines the `xlink:show` attribute to be `replace`, which means that if the user activates the link, it will replace the current document with the image file referenced on line 5.
- Line 8 defines the `xlink:role` attribute to be `image`.
- Line 9 defines the `xlink:title` attribute to be `"A map image"`.
- Line 10 specifies the text for the link, which will be clickable in a browser window.
- Line 11 contains the ending tag for the <map> linking element.

As a final example, let's change the value of the `xlink:actuate` attribute on line 6 to `onLoad`:

```
1  <?xml version="1.0"?>
2  <map
3     xmlns:xlink="http://www.w3.org/1999/xlink"
4     xlink:type="simple"
5     xlink:href="mapimage.gif"
6     xlink:actuate="onLoad"
7     xlink:show="replace"
8     xlink:role="image"
9     xlink:title="A map image">
10    Link to Map image
11 </map>
```

Change value of `xlink:actuate` attribute to `onLoad`.

This code modifies the behavior of the link so that the link is automatically followed when the page loads. Because the value of the `xlink:show` attribute in line 7 is `replace`, the browser automatically loads the image file that is referenced in line 5 into the browser window as soon as the XML file is opened, and it replaces the XML file in the window. Figure 6.4 shows the result of opening this file.

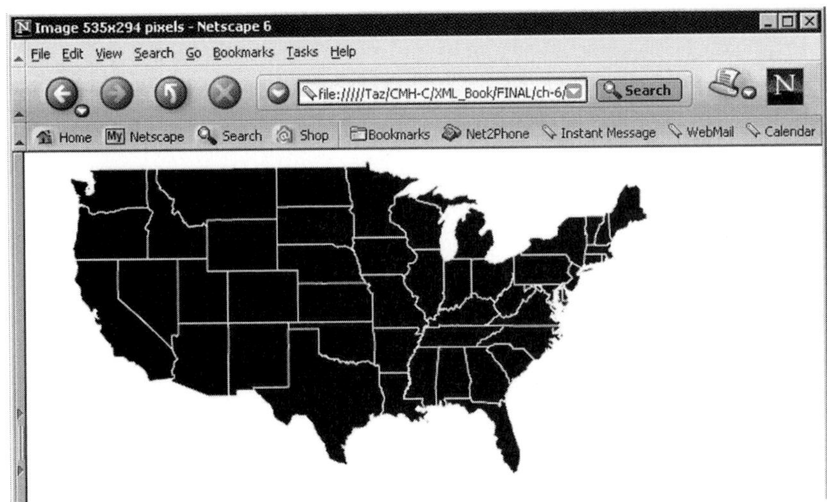

Figure 6.4 XLink Example in Netscape 6 (`mapimage.gif`) with the `onLoad` Value Set for the `xlink:actuate` Attribute

Defining a Simple Link in a DTD

If you use a DTD for your XML document, you must define the attributes for a linking element in the DTD. Let's look at the DTDs for the two previous examples. Following is an XML document with the DTD, and the XML code from the first example:

```
<?xml version="1.0" standalone="yes"?>
<!DOCTYPE map [
   <!ELEMENT map (#PCDATA)>
   <!ATTLIST map
   xmlns:xlink  CDATA   #FIXED   "http://www.w3.org/1999/xlink"
   xlink:type   CDATA   #FIXED   "simple"
   xlink:href   CDATA   #REQUIRED>
]>
<map
   xmlns:xlink="http://www.w3.org/1999/xlink"
   xlink:type="simple"
   xlink:href="mapimage.gif">
   Link to Map image
</map>
```

DTD declarations for XLink attributes

Following is an explanation of the relevant lines in the DTD:

- Line 3 contains the element declaration for the <map> element.
- Line 4 begins the attribute list for the <map> element.
- Line 5 declares the namespace. Because there is only one valid namespace for XLink, this value can be fixed in the DTD.
- Line 6 defines the `xlink:type` attribute to be a fixed value of `simple`.
- Line 7 defines the `xlink:href` attribute to be a required attribute.

> ☆ **SHORTCUT** You can define any of the attributes in the DTD as fixed, depending on the requirements of the program. If an attribute is defined as fixed, the program will automatically include that attribute when processing the document, so there is no need to include the attribute in the XML document itself.

Because the namespace and `xlink:type` attributes in lines 5 and 6 are fixed, you can omit them from the XML document. Following is the new document without the fixed attributes:

```
1  <?xml version="1.0" standalone="yes"?>
2  <!DOCTYPE map [
3     <!ELEMENT map (#PCDATA)>
4     <!ATTLIST map
5        xmlns:xlink CDATA   #FIXED "http://www.w3.org/1999/xlink"
6        xlink:type  CDATA   #FIXED "simple"
7        xlink:href  CDATA   #REQUIRED>
8  ]>
9  <map xlink:href="mapimage.gif">Link to Map image</map>
```

Declaring these fixed attributes in the DTD allows you to omit redundancy and produce much cleaner code. When the fixed pieces of information are omitted, the syntax for this <map> element in line 9 looks very much like the HTML <a> link syntax shown at the beginning of the chapter.

Let's look at the DTD for the second sample XML document. Here is the document with the DTD and additional attribute declarations.

```
<?xml version="1.0" standalone="yes"?>
<!DOCTYPE map [
   <!ELEMENT map (#PCDATA)>
   <!ATTLIST map
      xmlns:xlink CDATA   #FIXED "http://www.w3.org/1999/xlink"
      xlink:type  CDATA   #FIXED "simple"
      xlink:href  CDATA   #REQUIRED
      xlink:show (replace| new| embed| other| none)   #IMPLIED
      xlink:actuate (onRequest| onLoad| other| none) #IMPLIED
      xlink:role  CDATA   #IMPLIED
      xlink:title CDATA   #IMPLIED>
]>
```

DTD declarations for XLink attributes for the <map> element

```
13 <map
14    xlink:href="mapimage.gif"
15    xlink:actuate="onRequest"
16    xlink:show="replace"
17    xlink:role="image"
18    xlink:title="A map image">
19    Link to Map image
20 </map>
```

Notice that the namespace declaration and the `xlink:type` attribute have again been omitted because they are defined as fixed in the DTD. Also notice that the declarations for `show` and `actuate` in lines 6 and 7 use enumerated lists to list the only valid values for these attributes. This ensures that the XML code adheres to the XLink recommendation. The values that are defined as `#IMPLIED` are optional in this DTD. However, you could define any of these attributes as `#REQUIRED` if you wanted to ensure their inclusion.

Extended Links

Extended links provide a much more complex linking structure in XML. The W3C XLink recommendation defines an **extended link** as "a link that associates an arbitrary number of resources." Extended links create relationships between and among many different resources and provide multiple ways of linking back and forth among those resources, making these types of links multidirectional.

Figure 6.5 shows the relationship of an extended link to multiple resources.

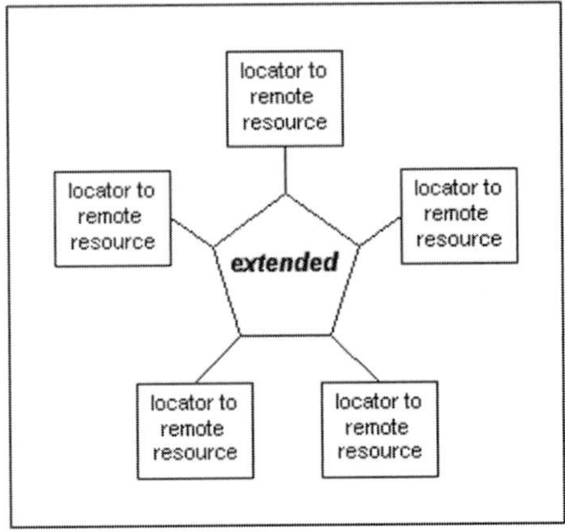

Figure 6.5 Extended XLink Relationship Model (from the W3C XLink Recommendation)

The syntax of an extended link is similar to that of a simple link. The value of the `xlink:type` attribute for an extended link is `extended`. Four other values can be set for the `xlink:type` attribute in extended links: `resource`, locator, arc, and title. These types further describe the extended linking element and its child elements.

Let's look at an example using one of these additional types, the <locator> element:

```
1  <courses  xmlns:xlink="http://www.w3.org/1999/xlink"
2            xlink:type="extended">
3     <locator xlink:type="locator"
4            xlink:href="courses/xml101.xml"
5            xlink:title="XML 101"/>
6     <locator xlink:type="locator"
7            xlink:href="courses/advxml.xml"
8            xlink:title="Advanced XML"/>
9     <locator xlink:type="locator"
10           xlink:href="courses/bw.xml"
11           xlink:title="Basket Weaving"/>
12    Link to Course
13 </courses>
```

The <courses> opening tag on lines 1 and 2 defines the XLink namespace and sets the link type to extended. Then three <locator> child elements are defined, starting on lines 3, 6, and 9. These <locator> elements define the target resources for this link. A <locator> element sets the value of the xlink:type attribute to the value locator to identify it as a target resource for this extended link. The xlink:href and xlink:title attributes have the same functions in extended links as they do in simple links. All the <locator> elements are empty elements in this example.

Unlike the examples in the previous section on simple links, this XLink example can link to three resources as opposed to only one. Extended links add a much more powerful means of connecting documents to one another. Unfortunately, as stated at the beginning of this chapter, they are not supported by either Internet Explorer or Netscape Web browser at the time of the writing of this book.

Defining an Extended Link in a DTD

The DTD declarations for an extended link are a bit more complex than for a simple link. Following is the XML document with the DTD declarations:

```
<?xml version="1.0" standalone="yes"?>
<!DOCTYPE map [
   <!ELEMENT courses (locator*, resource*, arc*, title?)>
   <!ATTLIST courses
      xmlns:xlink    CDATA    #FIXED
                              "http://www.w3.org/1999/xlink"
      xlink:type     CDATA    #FIXED      "extended">
   <!ELEMENT locator EMPTY>
   <!ATTLIST locator
      xlink:href     CDATA    #REQUIRED
      xlink:title    CDATA    #IMPLIED>
```

DTD declarations for XLink attributes for the <courses> element.

DTD declarations for XLink attributes for the <locator> elements.

```
11 ]>
12 <courses xmlns:xlink="http://www.w3.org/1999/xlink"
13                           xlink:type="extended">
14    <locator xlink:type="locator"
15                           xlink:href="courses/xml101.xml"
16                           xlink:title="XML 101"/>
17    <locator xlink:type="locator"
18                           xlink:href="courses/advxml.xml"
19                           xlink:title="Advanced XML"/>
20    <locator xlink:type="locator"
21                           xlink:href="courses/bw.xml"
22                           xlink:title="Basket Weaving"/>
23 </courses>
```

Following is an explanation of the relevant lines in the DTD:

- Line 3 defines the `<courses>` element to contain zero or more `<locator>`, `<resource>`, or `<arc>` child elements, and exactly zero or one `<title>` element.
- Line 4 begins the attribute declaration for the `<courses>` element.
- Lines 5 and 6 declare the namespace as fixed, and the `xlink:type` value as `extended`.
- Line 7 defines the element `<locator>` to be an empty element.
- Line 8 begins the attribute declaration for the `<locator>` element.
- Lines 9 and 10 define the attributes for the `<locator>` element. The `xlink:href` attribute is required, and the `xlink:title` attribute is optional.

TIP XPath and XPointer

XPath and XPointer are two XML technologies developed by the W3C to extend linking functionality in XML. They allow linking to certain parts of a document based on the document hierarchy. These topics are beyond the scope of this book. For more information, see "Online References" at the end of the chapter.

Summary

- A hyperlink, or link, is an area of a Web page on which visitors can click to move to a related resource, such as another Web page or a file.
- The XLink specification takes much of its syntax from the syntax of HTML links because of their popularity and ease of use.
- XLinks in XML are much more powerful than links in HTML. For example, they allow you to create links for any element, not just a few pre-defined elements, and they allow you to link to multiple resources.
- XLink simple links are very similar to HTML links. Simple links can link to only one target resource and are unidirectional. To be valid, they require the `type` and `href` attributes. If an XML document uses a DTD, the XLink attributes must be declared in the DTD. Attributes that are declared as `#FIXED` in the DTD do not need to be included in the XML code of the document, thus allowing XML authors to create cleaner code.
- XLink extended links can link to multiple target resources and can be multidirectional.

Online References

W3C XLink Recommendation
`http://www.w3.org/XML/Linking`

XLink Reference—XML.com
`http://www.xml.com/pub/a/2000/09/xlink/part2.html`

XML Linking Implementations—Browser Compatibility Chart
`http://www.w3.org/XML/2000/09/LinkingImplementations.html`

XLink: An Introductory Example—XML.com
`http://www.xml.com/pub/a/2000/09/xlink/part1.html`

XLink Basics—An On-Line Tutorial
`http://www.melonfire.com/community/columns/trog/article.php?id=90`

XML Linking and Addressing Languages—XML Cover Pages
`http://xml.coverpages.org/xll.html`

Initial Experiences of an XLink Implementation
`http://xml.coverpages.org/carr-xlinkexperience.html`

XML Path Language (XPath) Recommendation
`http://www.w3.org/TR/xpath`

XML Pointer Language (XPointer) Candidate Recommendation
`http://www.w3.org/TR/xptr/`

☆Review Questions

1. What is the difference between simple and extended links in the XLink specification?
2. What are the two required attributes for simple links?
3. Which XML elements can be links?
4. Which XLink attribute determines when the link is activated?
5. What are the five possible values for the `show` attribute in a simple link?
6. If an XML document uses a DTD, do the XLink attributes need to be included?
7. What are the five values that can be assigned to the `type` attribute for extended links?
8. What is the role of the `<locator>` element in an extended link?

☆Hands-On Exercises

1. Following are three HTML links. Create the equivalent XML simple links. You can name your elements anything you like. Assume that the target resources will replace the current page in the browser window.

```
1 <a href="http://www.chughes.com/boating.html">
  Link to Boating site</a>
2 <img src="images/button.gif">
3 <a href="boating.html"><img src="images/boating.gif">
  </a>
```

2. Create an XML document containing the links you created in Exercise 1, and test your links in a Netscape 6 browser.
3. Create the DTD entry for the following element. Use the `#FIXED` attribute for the namespace and `xlink:type` attributes.

```
<magazine
  xmlns:xlink="http://www.w3.org/1999/xlink"
  xlink:type="simple"
  xlink:href="magazine.xml"
  xlink:actuate="onRequest"
  xlink:show="new"
  xlink:title="Magazine">
  Link to Magazine document
</map>
```

4. Assume that the `<magazine>` element from Exercise 3 has three articles associated with it. Create the extended link to include `<locator>` elements to the following documents: `article-1.xml`, `article-2.xml`, and `article-3.xml`.
5. Create the DTD for the extended link you created in Exercise 5.

New XML Technologies: XSL Style Sheets and XML Schemas

XSL style sheets and XML schemas are two exciting new XML technologies that extend the functionality of XML and provide developers with XML-based alternatives to CSS style sheets and DTDs. Because they are new technologies, few programs support them yet. Both technologies are complex, and this chapter provides a brief introduction to each.

Chapter Objectives

- To understand the importance of XSL style sheets and XML schemas
- To learn about the two components of XSL style sheets: XSL Formatting Objects and XSL Transformations
- To learn about the two components of XML schema: datatypes and structures

The Importance of XSL Style Sheets and XML Schemas

You learned a little bit about XSL style sheets and XML schema technologies in Chapters Three and Four. They are new members of the XML family of technologies, and both recommendations were released by the W3C in 2001. They are both XML namespaces, which you learned about in Chapter Five.

As of the writing of this book, these technologies are so new that you won't find many working implementations of them in programs, such as Web browsers. But style sheets and schemas promise to be important XML technologies, becoming even more important in the future as they are integrated into Web browsers and other programs. This chapter gives you a brief introduction to each of these technologies. The details are beyond the scope of this book, but by the end of this chapter you should have a good understanding of the basics of each technology and the ways they are used.

Overview of XSL Style Sheets

The Extensible Stylesheet Language (XSL) was released as a recommendation by the W3C in October 2001. The specification consists of two main parts:

- XSL Formatting Objects (XSL-FO): an XML vocabulary for specifying formatting semantics
- XSL Transformations (XSLT): a language for transforming XML documents.

In Chapter Four, you learned how to use Cascading Style Sheets (CSS) to format XML documents to be viewed in a Web browser. XSL style sheets follow a similar process. The Formatting Objects portion of the recommendation defines the properties that can be used to format a document, such as font size and color, and the XSLT portion defines the transformation process.

For example, this book has used Internet Explorer to display sample XML files. When you open an XML file in Internet Explorer that does not have a specific style sheet declared, the browser uses a default XSL style sheet that comes with its XML parser, MSXML. This style sheet displays the XML file with the specific colors for the element names, and it uses the "+" and "-" sign functions to expand and collapse the elements.

SHORTCUT You can see the XSL style sheet that is a part of the MSXML parser that ships with Internet Explorer. This style sheet is used to format XML documents in the Internet Explorer browser. Type the following into the Address box in Internet Explorer:

```
res://msxml.dll/defaultss.xsl
```

XSL, like CSS, is a language used for describing the format, or presentation, of XML documents. However, XSL is written as an XML language, and it was developed specifically for use with XML documents. XSL also offers many additional features and functions that are not available with CSS, such as the ability to transform XML documents to other formats using XSLT. Because XSL and its components are new, it has not yet been widely implemented.

XSL Formatting Objects (XSL-FO)

XSL Formatting Objects is part of the XSL recommendation that was released by the W3C in October 2001. The properties of XSL-FO are similar to the properties of CSS style sheets. XSL-FO allows you to define values for text properties, such as font size and color, border widths and heights, and so on. XSL-FO also provides a number of advanced options. These advanced options are beyond the scope of this book but are well documented online.

The namespace for XSL Formatting Objects is `http://www.w3.org/1999/XSL/Format`. It is declared on the `<fo:root>` element:

```
<fo:root xmlns:fo="http://www.w3.org/1999/Format">
```

Let's look at a simple example. Here is how to format a piece of text—with a font size of 12 points, font color of red, and aligned to the left—using XSL-FO:

```
1  <fo:block
2     font-size="12pt"
3     font-color="red"
4     text-align="left">
5     Block of text...
6  </fo:block>
```

Line 1 begins the formatting rule with an `<fo:block>` element. This element is usually used to format text. Lines 2–4 define the various attributes and values of the formatting properties. Line 5 contains the text to format, and line 6 ends the rule. Unfortunately, none of the current browsers yet support XSL-FO. Other programs, however, are available, such as FOP (Formatting Objects Processor). This free Java program takes an XML file and XSL-FO style sheet as input and creates an output file. FOP currently supports a number of output formats, including Portable Document Format (PDF) and text. "Online References" at the end of the chapter lists URLs where you can download and try FOP. Appendix A provides information and URLs for additional tools.

XSL Transformations (XSLT)

XSLT, the most widely used implementation of XSL, has been around for quite a while. The recommendation for XSLT was released by the W3C in November 1999, a few years before the finalized recommendation for XSL. XSLT is used to **transform**, or convert, an XML document into other document formats, including other XML documents, HTML documents, or PDF files. Figure 7.1, taken from the W3C's recommendation for XSLT, shows how XSLT works.

With tree transformation, the structure of the result tree can be quite different from the structure of the source tree.

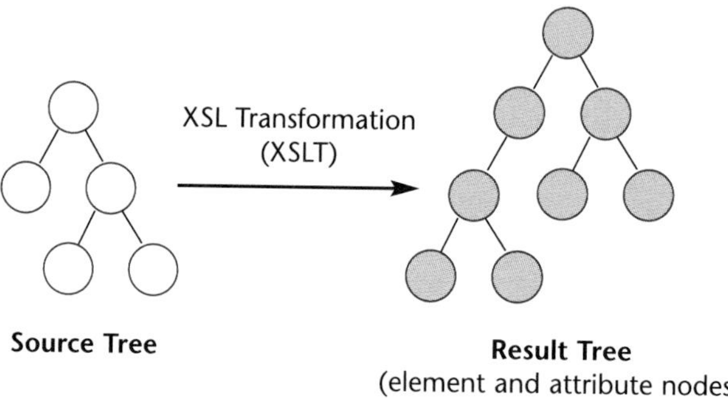

In constructing the result tree, the source tree can be filtered and reordered, and arbitrary structure and generated content can be added.

Figure 7.1 XSLT Transformation Process (from the W3C Recommendation)

The namespace for XSLT Formatting Objects is `http://www.w3.org/1999/XSL/Transform` and is declared on the `<xsl:stylesheet>` element:

```
<xsl:stylesheet version="1.0"
xmlns:xsl="http://www.w3.org/1999/XSL/Transform">
```

The `version` attribute states which version of XSLT this style sheet uses—in this case, `1.0`.

To use XSLT, you must use a program that supports XSL transformations. The examples in this section use Internet Explorer 6.

☆ **WARNING** Because the XSL specification is new, only the newest browser versions support XSL style sheets. To view this chapter's examples and to complete the exercises, you must use version 6 or later of Internet Explorer or Netscape. The earlier versions do not support XSLT.

To use XSLT, you need three things:

- A source XML file
- An XSLT style sheet
- A program that supports XSLT

Let's look at an example of how to use XSLT to transform an XML document into HTML. Suppose that you have an XML file that contains information about classic cars, and you would like to display it on the Web as a table. Following is the XML file that you want to transform. Figure 7.2 shows this XML document in Internet Explorer without a style sheet.

```
<?xml version="1.0"?>
<inventory>
   <vehicle>
      <make>Chevy</make>
      <model>Camaro</model>
      <color>Blue</color>
      <year>1968</year>
      <mileage>52,000</mileage>
      <price>$18,000</price>
   </vehicle>
   <vehicle>
      <make>Ford</make>
      <model>Mustang</model>
      <color>Chrome</color>
      <year>1965</year>
      <mileage>12,000</mileage>
      <price>$30,000</price>
   </vehicle>
   <vehicle>
      <make>Jaguar</make>
      <model>Roadster</model>
      <color>Red</color>
      <year>1967</year>
      <mileage>76,000</mileage>
      <price>$23,000</price>
   </vehicle>
   <vehicle>
      <make>Porsche</make>
      <model>911</model>
      <year>1970</year>
      <color>Black</color>
      <mileage>8,000</mileage>
      <price>$35,000</price>
   </vehicle>
</inventory>
```

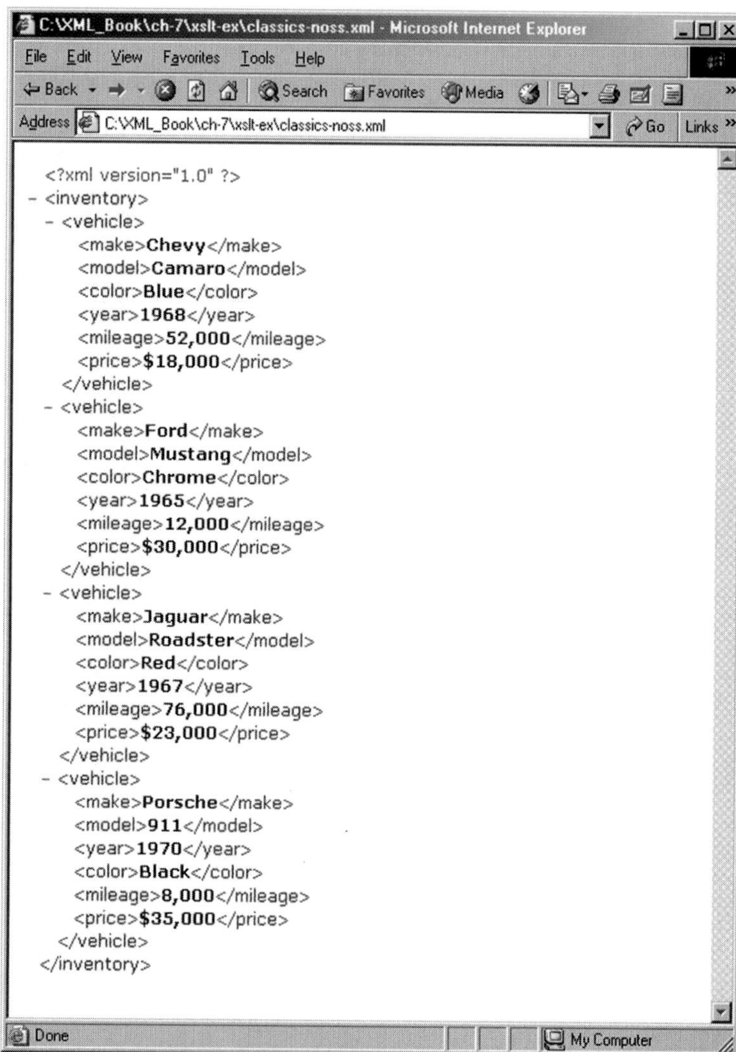

Figure 7.2 Classic Cars XML Document in Internet Explorer

Following is the XSL style sheet that we will use to transform the XML document into HTML.

```
1  <?xml version="1.0"?>
2  <xsl:stylesheet version="1.0"
      xmlns:xsl="http://www.w3.org/1999/XSL/Transform">
3  <xsl:template match="/">
4  <html>
5     <body bgcolor="white">
6        <table border="2" cellpadding="5"
               bgcolor="cyan">
7           <tr>
8               <th>Make and Model</th>
9               <th>Color</th>
10              <th>Year</th>
11              <th>Mileage</th>
12              <th>Price</th>
13          </tr>
14          <xsl:for-each select="inventory/vehicle">
15          <tr>
16              <td><xsl:value-of select="make"/>
17                  <xsl:value-of select="model"/></td>
18              <td><xsl:value-of select="color"/></td>
19              <td><xsl:value-of select="year"/></td>
20              <td><xsl:value-of select="mileage"/></td>
21              <td><xsl:value-of select="price"/></td>
22          </tr>
23          </xsl:for-each>
24       </table>
25    </body>
26 </html>
27 </xsl:template>
28 </xsl:stylesheet>
```

XSL template

for-each loop

It is possible to define many style sheets for one document. This style sheet consists of only single formatting template, which begins on line 3 and ends on line 27. The **formatting template** determines how to format the XML document. We are using HTML to provide the formatting information for display in a Web browser. If you were using an XSL style sheet to format the document for some other type of output, such as a PDF file or print, you would use a different method of formatting for the template.

This template also contains an `<xsl:for-each>` **looping** instruction element that begins on line 14 and ends on line 23. This XSL instruction tells the processor to find each instance of the `select` attribute value—in this case, `inventory/vehicle`—and format the elements based on the style sheet instructions contained between the open and end `<xsl:for-each>` tags. Within the loop are five additional `<xsl:value-of>` elements, which tell the processor to look for additional elements. The value of the `select` attribute for each of the <xsl:value-of> elements defines which element that particular element is looking for. In this example, the loop **iterates** over each of the classic cars in the XML file and creates one row in the HTML table to display that car's information.

Given these instructions, the processor looks for all <vehicle> elements, which are child elements of the <inventory> element, in the Classic Car XML file. It then creates one row in the HTML table for each car's information. The loop continues until all the <vehicle> elements have been found or until it reaches the ending </inventory> tag. Any <vehicle> element that is found after the </inventory> ending tag will not be processed using these instructions because the instruction specifically tells the processor to look only for <vehicle> elements that are child elements of the <inventory> element.

Following is a line-by-line explanation of this style sheet:

- Line 1 is the XML declaration.
- In line 2, the namespace declaration for the XSL style sheet is declared on the <xsl:stylesheet> element. The declaration also states that this version of XSL is version `1.0`.
- Line 3 begins the <xsl:template> element. The `match` attribute has a value of /, which means that this template will match on literal values, meaning that the processor will match the values of the `select` attributes to the actual element names in the XML document.
- Line 4 of the template begins the HTML document with the opening <html> HTML tag.
- Line 5 of the template begins the body of the HTML document with the opening <body> HTML tag.
- Line 6 of the template begins the HTML <table> element and defines formatting properties for the table.
- Line 7 of the template begins the first row of the table.
- Line 8 of the template defines the column heading for the first column of the table, "Make and Model."
- Line 9 of the template defines the column heading for the second column of the table, "Color."
- Line 10 of the template defines the column heading for the third column of the table, "Year."
- Line 11 of the template defines the column heading for the fourth column of the table, "Mileage."
- Line 12 of the template defines the column heading for the fifth column of the table, "Price."
- Line 13 of the template ends the first row of the table.
- Line 14 of the template is the beginning of the <xsl:for-each> loop.

- Line 15 of the template begins a new row.
- Line 16 of the template opens the first table cell in the row and looks for the `<make>` element value for the current `<vehicle>` element.
- Line 17 of the template looks for the `<model>` element value for the current `<vehicle>` element and closes the table cell.
- Line 18 of the template opens the second table cell in the row, looks for the `<color>` element value for the current `<vehicle>` element, and then ends the table cell.
- Line 19 of the template opens the third table cell in the row, looks for the `<year>` element value for the current `<vehicle>` element, and then ends the table cell.
- Line 20 of the template opens the fourth table cell in the row, looks for the `<mileage>` element value for the current `<vehicle>` element, and then ends the table cell.
- Line 21 of the template opens the fifth table cell in the row, looks for the `<price>` element value for the current `<vehicle>` element, and then ends the table cell.
- Line 22 of the template ends the current row.
- Line 23 of the template ends the `<xsl:for-each>` loop. If there are additional `<vehicle>` elements to process, the XML processor returns to line 14 and processes the next `<vehicle>` element. This repeats until there are no more `<vehicle>` elements to be processed.
- Line 24 of the template ends the HTML `<table>` element that started on line 6.
- Line 25 of the template ends the HTML `<body>` element that started on line 5.
- Line 26 of the template ends the HTML `<html>` element that started on line 4.
- Line 27 ends the `<xsl:template>` element.
- Line 28 ends the style sheet.

TIP For style sheets that have only a single template, the `match` attribute for the `<xsl:template>` element on line 3 is equal to /, which means to simply match literal values and not to look for complex pattern-matching algorithms. **Pattern matching** allows a program to look for patterns in a set or stream of data. Other values for the `match` attribute allow you to search for certain pieces of information or element names based on a pattern. This function makes XSL extremely powerful. The W3C's recommendations for XSL and XSLT provide detailed information on how to use pattern matching.

To view the Classic Car XML document using the style sheet, we must add the style sheet declaration to the XML file. Here are the first few lines of the XML file with the declaration:

```
1  <?xml version="1.0"?>
2  <?xml-stylesheet type="text/xsl" href="inventory.xls"?>
3  <inventory>
4     <vehicle>
5        <make>Chevy</make>
```

XSL style sheet declaration

The style sheet declaration is on line 2. Notice that it looks very similar to the CSS style sheet declaration that you learned in Chapter Four. But here, the value of the `type` attribute is `text/xsl`, compared with `text/css` for a CSS style sheet. The style sheet can be located on the local machine or on the Internet, as defined by the value of the `href` attribute.

Now that you have linked the style sheet with the XML document, you can view the XML file in Internet Explorer. Figure 7.3 shows the XML file in Internet Explorer formatted with the style sheet.

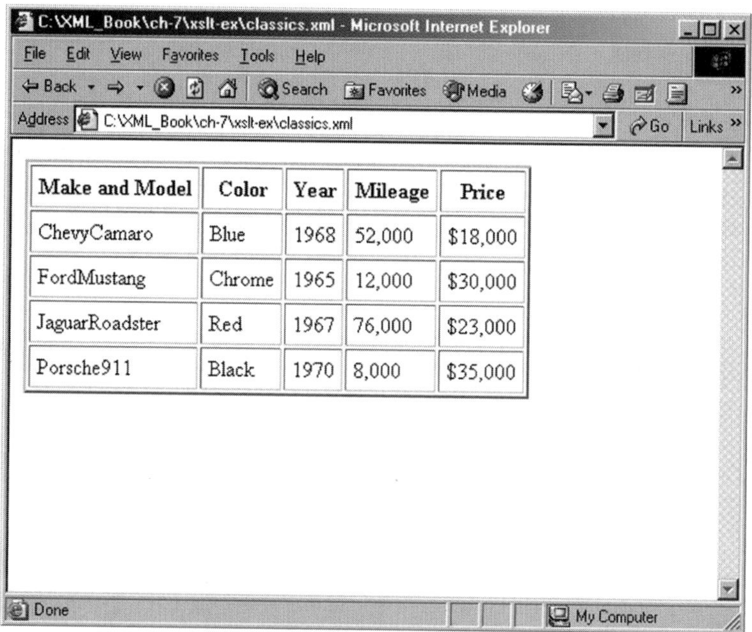

Make and Model	Color	Year	Mileage	Price
ChevyCamaro	Blue	1968	52,000	$18,000
FordMustang	Chrome	1965	12,000	$30,000
JaguarRoadster	Red	1967	76,000	$23,000
Porsche911	Black	1970	8,000	$35,000

Figure 7.3 XML File Formatted with XSL Style Sheet in Internet Explorer

☆ **SHORTCUT** Try this example yourself by doing the following:

1. Create an XML file called `classics.xml` using the XML file shown earlier. Be sure to include the XSL style sheet declaration.
2. Create a style sheet file called `inventory.xsl` using the sample style sheet.
3. Save both files in the same directory on your hard drive.
4. Open the `classics.xml` file in Internet Explorer 6 or later to see the results.

Overview of XML Schemas

The XML Schema specification, released by the W3C as a recommendation in May 2001, consists of two parts:

- Part I—XML Schema: Structures. This specification consists of a definition language for describing and constraining the content of XML documents.
- Part II—XML Schema: Datatypes. This specification defines the datatypes to be used in XML schemas.

XML **schemas**, like DTDs (see Chapter Three), are used to describe the structure of an XML document. An XSL schema definition specifies which elements and attributes are valid for a certain document type, and which elements and attributes are required and optional.

When you use an XML schema, you must declare namespaces in both the XML document and the XML schema document. The namespace for the XML schema document is `http://www.w3.org/2001/XMLSchema` and is declared as follows:

```
<xsd:schema xmlns:xsd="http://www.w3.org/2001/XMLSchema">
```

When an XML file uses an XML schema to define its valid format, it is said to be an **instance document** of that schema. The namespace declaration declared on an element called `<products>` would look like this:

```
<product
   xmlns:xsi = "http://www.w3.org/2001/XMLSchema-instance"
   xsi:noNamespaceSchemaLocation = "product_schema.xsd">
```

This declaration declares the namespace to be `http://www.w3.org/2001/XMLSchema-instance`. This namespace is used for instance documents of XML schemas. The value of the second attribute, `xsi:noNamespaceSchemaLocation`, indicates where the schema document resides. This link can be on the local machine or anywhere on the Internet; in this case, it is on the local machine. This attribute indicates that there is no target namespace and that the prefix will not be used to indicate that an element belongs to the namespace. By default, each element defined in the schema is part of the namespace. This is the most common declaration for XML schemas.

If you wanted to declare an explicit namespace, you would use the following declaration:

```
<product
   xmlns:xsi = "http://www.w3.org/2001/XMLSchema-instance"
   xsi:schemaLocation="http://www.chughes.com/schemas/
Product product_schema.xsd">
```

The namespace for the instance document is the same, but now you use the `xsi:schemaLocation` attribute. The value of this attribute has two pieces. The first piece is the name of the namespace (`http://www.chughes.com/schemas/Product`), and the second piece is the schema file (`product_schema.xsd`). There is a space between these two values in the declaration.

TIP The XML Schema specification contains many more components than are presented in this chapter, including attribute declarations, attribute groupings, data filtering using pattern matching, and ways to use pattern matching to create your own datatypes. For more about XML schemas, see "Online References" at the end of the chapter.

XML Schema Datatypes

A number of simple datatypes are built into the XML Schema specification. Developers can also create their own datatypes based on the simple datatypes for specific functions, such as a part identification number. Following are some of the commonly used built-in simple datatypes. "Online References" at the end of the chapter shows where you can find the complete list.

- Integer
- String
- Date
- Time
- Float
- Byte
- ID
- IDREF

XML Schema Occurrence Constraints

Occurrence constraints define the number of times a particular element can or must occur. These constraints appear as attributes of an element. The minimum number of times an element can occur is set by the `minOccurs` attribute, and the maximum number is set by the `maxOccurs` attribute. The default value for each of these attributes is 1. You can set `maxOccurs` to the value `unbounded`, which indicates that there is no maximum number of occurrences for that element. You will see how to use these attributes in the example in the following section.

XML Schema Syntax

XML schema documents are written in XML and follow all the syntax rules you have learned so far about XML. Schema definitions for elements are divided into two types: simple types and complex types. **Simple** types describe elements that do not have any child elements. Simple types are written as empty elements in the schema document. **Complex** element types can contain child elements and attributes.

☆**WARNING** All elements that have child elements or attributes must use the complex type syntax to define the valid formats. If a document with only one element has attributes for that element, you must use the complex type syntax.

Example 1: Simple Type

Let's look at an example of a very simple XML document:

```
<?xml version="1.0"?>
<email
  xmlns:xsi = "http://www.w3.org/2001/XMLSchema-instance"
  xsi:noNamespaceSchemaLocation = "email_schema.xsd">
  This is my e-mail message
</email>
```

This document contains one element that does not have any child elements. Following is the schema for this document, email_schema.xsd:

```
1 <?xml version="1.0"?>
2 <xsd:schema xmlns:xsd="http://www.w3.org/2001/XMLSchema">
3    <xsd:element name="email" type="xsd:string"/>
4 </xsd:schema>
```

Following is a line-by-line explanation of this schema:

- Line 1 is the XML declaration.
- Line 2 is the namespace declaration for the root element, `<xsd:schema>`.
- Line 3 defines the format for the root element, `<email>`, and is an empty element. The value of the `name` attribute is the name of the element—in this case, `email`. The `type` attribute defines the datatype of the element—in this case, a string. Notice that the `xsd` prefix is also added to the value of the `type` element, `xsd:string`. This defines the datatype `xsd:string` as part of the schema namespace, thereby preventing confusion in case there is another use of "string" elsewhere in the document.
- Line 4 ends the `<xsd:schema>` element.

Example 2: Complex Type

Following is an XML document in which the root element, <message>, has child elements:

```
<?xml version="1.0"?>
<message
   xmlns:xsi = "http://www.w3.org/2001/XMLSchema-instance"
   xsi:noNamespaceSchemaLocation = "message_schema.xsd">
      <to>Joe Poller</to>
      <from>Brenda Lane</from>
      <date_sent/>
      <subject>Order 10011</subject>
      <body>
         Joe,
         Please let me know if order number 10011 has shipped.
         Thanks,
         Brenda
      </body>
</message>
```

This document contains a more complex element structure. Following is the schema for this document:

```
1  <?xml version="1.0"?>
2  <xsd:schema xmlns:xsd="http://www.w3.org/2001/XMLSchema">
3     <xsd:element name="message">
4        <xsd:complexType>
5           <xsd:sequence>
6              <xsd:element name="to" type="xsd:string"
                            minOccurs="1" maxOccurs="unbounded"/>
7              <xsd:element name="from" type="xsd:string"
                            minOccurs="1"/>
8              <xsd:element name="date_sent" type="xsd:date"/>
9              <xsd:element name="subject" type="xsd:string"/>
10             <xsd:element name="body" type="xsd:string"/>
11          </xsd:sequence>
12       </xsd:complexType>
13    </xsd:element>
14 </xsd:schema>
```

Following is a line-by-line explanation of this schema:

- Line 1 is the XML declaration.
- Line 2 is the namespace declaration for the root element, <xsd:schema>.
- Line 3 defines the root element, <message>. Notice that this element is not defined as an empty element because it has child elements that are defined

later. The element declaration ends on line 13. The child elements are all declared as empty elements.

- Line 4 defines the element as a `complexType` definition.
- In line 5, the `<xsd:sequence>` declaration allows you to control the order in which the elements appear in the XML document.
- Line 6 defines the element `<to>` with a datatype of `xsd:string` and as an empty element. The `minOccurs` attribute is set to `1`, which means that there must be at least one occurrence of this element. The `maxOccurs` attribute sets the maximum number of the `<to>` element to `unbounded`, which means that there is no maximum number of times this element can occur.
- Line 7 defines the element `<from>` with a datatype of `xsd:string` and as an empty element. The `minOccurs` attribute sets the minimum number of occurrences of the `<from>` element to `1`.
- Line 8 defines the element `<date>` with a datatype of `xsd:date` and as an empty element.
- Line 9 defines the element `<subject>` with a datatype of `xsd:string` and as an empty element.
- Line 10 defines the element `<body>` with a datatype of `xsd:string` and as an empty element
- Line 11 ends the `<xsd:sequence>` element that started on line 5.
- Line 12 ends the `<xsd:complexType>` element that started on line 4.
- Line 13 ends the `<xsd:element>` element that started on line 3.
- Line 14 ends the `<xsd:schema>` element that started on line 2.

Summary

- XSL style sheets and XML schemas are XML namespaces. Because these technologies are new, there is limited support for them in current programs.
- XSL style sheets consist of two components: XSL Formatting Objects and XSL Transformations. XSL-FO is an XML vocabulary for specifying formatting semantics, and XSLT is a language for transforming XML documents into other document types. One use of XSLT is to transform XML documents into HTML documents.
- There are two types of XML schemas: simple and complex. The XML Schema specification consists of two components: datatypes and structures. XML schemas have a number of built-in datatypes, or developers can create their own datatypes. Constraints can be applied to elements in an XML schema, such as sequence order of elements or the minimum and maximum occurrences of the elements within a document.

Online References

W3C XSL Specification
`http://www.w3.org/TR/xsl/`

W3C XSLT Specification
`http://www.w3.org/TR/xslt`

Hands-On XSL—IBM
`http://www-106.ibm.com/developerworks/library/hands-on-xsl/`

XSL Tutorial—W3 Schools
`http://www.w3schools.com/xsl/`

XSLT Tools and Editors
`http://www.xslt.com/xslt_tools_editors.html`

What Is XSL?
`http://www.w3.org/Style/XSL/WhatIsXSL.html`

XML Schema
`http://www.w3.org/XML/Schema`

XML Schema Part 1: Structures
`http://www.w3.org/TR/xmlschema-1`

XML Schema Part 2: Datatypes
`http://www.w3.org/TR/xmlschema-2`

XML Schema-A Brief Introduction
`http://lucas.ucs.ed.ac.uk/xml-schema/`

☆Review Questions

1. What is the namespace for XSLT?
2. What is the namespace for XSL-FO?
3. Which component of XSL defines formatting properties for displaying elements?
4. What is an XSL template?
5. Describe what a for-each loop within an XSL template does.
6. What is the namespace for XML Schema?
7. List three of the XML Schema built-in datatypes.
8. What value would you set the `maxOccurs` attribute to in an XML schema if you wanted the number of elements that can occur within a document to be unlimited?
9. What is the difference between simple and complex XML schema types?

☆Hands-On Exercises

1. Create the XSL-FO formatting rule for a piece of text with a font size of 24 and a font color of blue.
2. Using the XSL style sheet from the Classic Cars example in this chapter, create a style sheet for the following XML document that will transform the document into a two-column HTML table (see Figure 7.4):

```
<?xml version="1.0"?>
   <state_capitals>
      <state>
         <name>Massachusetts</name>
         <capital>Boston</capital>
      </state>
      <state>
         <name>New York</name>
         <capital>Albany</capital>
      </state>
      <state>
         <name>Ohio</name>
         <capital>Columbus</capital>
      </state>
      <state>
         <name>Georgia</name>
         <capital>Atlanta</capital>
      </state>
   </state_capitals>
```

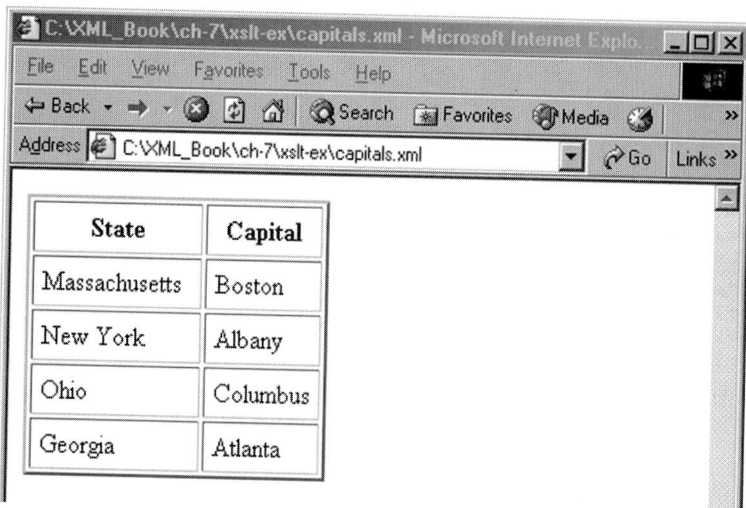

Figure 7.4 Two-column Table Version of Classic Cars Data

3. Save the XML file and XSL style sheet from Exercise 2 to your hard drive, and display the XML table in an XSL-compliant browser.
4. Create a simple-type XML schema document for the following XML document:

```
<?xml version="1.0"?>
<company>
  Joe's House of Pizza
</company>
```

5. Create a complex-type XML schema document for the following XML document:

```
<?xml version="1.0"?>
<company>
  <name>Joe's House of Pizza</name>
  <address>265 Sunbury Ln.</address>
  <city>Orlando</city>
  <state>Florida</state>
  <zip>11111</zip>
</company>
```

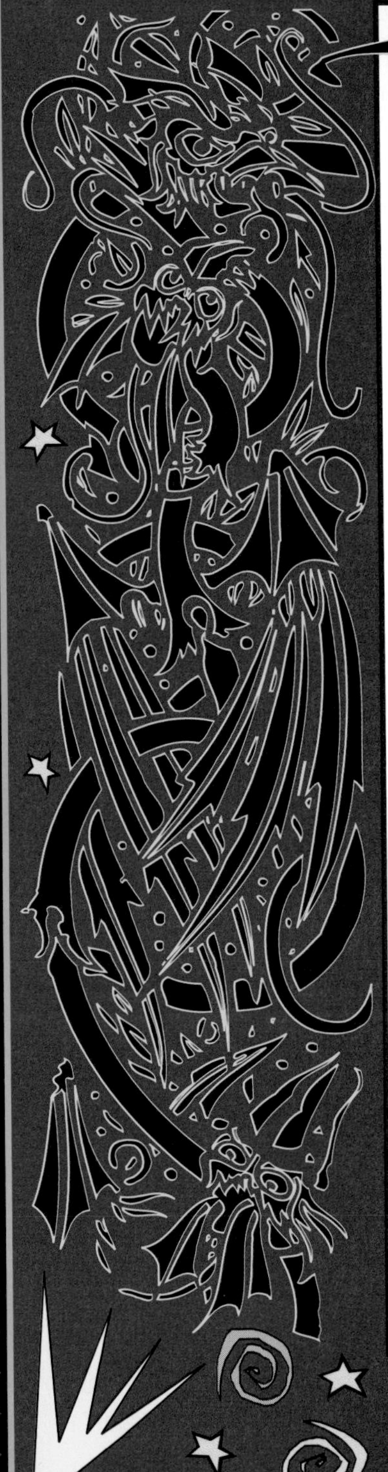

CHAPTER EIGHT

XML Programs and Programming

Throughout this book you have learned about the syntax of XML and various associated technologies. But what can you do with your XML document after you have created it? This chapter presents an overview of some of the ways you can put XML technologies to work.

Chapter Objectives

- To understand the use of XML with various programs
- To learn about XML parsers
- To study the basics of the Document Object Model (DOM)
- To learn about the Simple Application Programming Interface for XML (SAX)
- To discover the differences between SAX and DOM
- To learn about using XML with programming languages
- To understand how to use XML with databases

- To look at a variety of available XML programs
- To study MathML, an XML-based language for math functions
- To learn about the future possibilities of XML

Programming with XML

Since the introduction of XML, hundreds of products have been developed for processing XML documents. In the beginning, most of the interfaces were developed differently, and it quickly became apparent that standards were needed to ease the job of developing XML tools and programs. You have already used one such program, an XML parser, to check the syntax of and validate your XML document and display it in a browser. The parser provided with a Web browser is only one type of program that can process XML documents.

In this chapter, you will learn about the programming standards being developed for use with XML. The details of these topics are beyond the scope of this book, so the purpose of this chapter is to provide an overview. For more information about the topics covered, see "Online References" at the end of this chapter.

XML Parsers

In Chapter Two, you learned that there are two types of XML parsers: validating and nonvalidating. Validating parsers check the syntax and validate an XML document against a document model, and nonvalidating parsers check only the syntax to verify that the document is well formed.

A parser is a program that takes an XML document as input, reads the elements and attributes, and checks to make sure that the document conforms to the rules of XML syntax. A validating parser goes one step further and checks to ensure that the document conforms to the document model that is associated with it. Parsers are code libraries written in a programming language such as Java, C++, or Perl. For example, the XML parser that comes with Internet Explorer is called the MSXML parser.

After the parser has checked the document, it is sent to an XML processor, which does something useful with it. In the case of a Web browser, it displays the document in the browser window. If a style sheet is associated with the document, the browser displays the document according to the formatting rules set forth in the style sheet. The browser program doesn't automatically "know" what to do with XML documents; it has been specifically programmed to process them in this way.

The examples in this book have used the Internet Explorer and Netscape Web browsers, but many other parsers are available. You can find more information about parsers in Appendix A.

The Document Object Model

The Document Object Model (DOM) is a W3C recommendation for advanced processing of HTML and XML documents. The DOM Level 1 recommendation was released by the W3C in October 1998. The W3C describes DOM as "a platform- and language-neutral interface that will allow programs and scripts to dynamically access and update the content, structure and style of documents. The document can be further processed and the results of that processing can be incorporated back into the presented page."

The recommendation is complex and currently contains three levels: Level 1, Level 2, and Level 3. Level 1 provides the core document models, Level 2 includes Level 1 and adds a model for style sheets, and Level 3 includes Level 1 and adds a model for content (DTD or schema). These levels are in various stages of development by the W3C. See "Online References" at the end of the chapter for links containing information about the different levels.

The concept behind DOM is simple. DOM takes an XML document as input and creates an object structure in memory, which can then be accessed by programs. DOM creates a tree-like structure, with branches and leaves to represent the hierarchy of the document.

Let's look at an example. Recall the tree diagram of the "Job Posting" document from Chapter One. Figure 8.1 shows the tree structure. Following is the code for this example:

```
<?xml version="1.0"?>
<job-posting>
   <title>Job Title: <emphasis>Web master</emphasis></title>
   <description>We are looking for a Web master to oversee
   the management of our company Web site. The Web master
   will be responsible for working with other staff members
   to collect information for the Web site, and for creating
   and maintaining the Web pages.</description>
   <skill-list>
      <skill>Basic writing skills</skill>
      <skill>good communication skills</skill>
      <skill>HTML</skill>
   </skill-list>
</job-posting>
```

DOM creates in memory a structure similar to the tree structure diagram in Figure 8.1 and then allows programs to access the various pieces. Each box in the diagram is called a **node**. A node is simply a piece of the XML document, such as an element, an attribute, an entity, a comment, or a text string (content). Each node can have siblings, ancestors, and descendants. The **root** node, called the Document Object, is the only node that does not have a parent node.

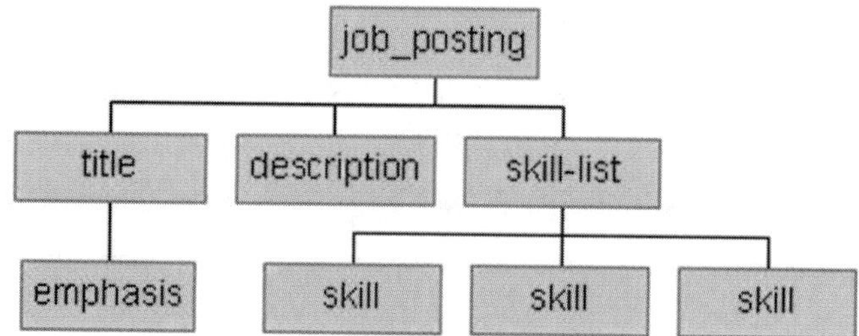

Figure 8.1 XML Tree Structure for "Job Posting"

An Example Using Microsoft's XMLDOM

Microsoft's DOM, the DOM that is used in Internet Explorer, includes an XML parser. This component is a COM component that is included with the Internet Explorer 5.0 and later Web browser. The following example uses this browser.

The Microsoft DOM includes the following components as nodes for its XML parser:

- XML declaration
- Element
- Attribute
- Entity reference (see Chapter Two)
- Comment
- Character data (CDATA)
- Parsed character data (PCDATA)
- The DTD declaration
- Namespaces
- White space
- Processing instructions

After the DOM has created the object, or tree structure, in memory, a program can access the various pieces as objects. Tables 8.1 and 8.2 show a partial list of Microsoft's DOM object properties and methods.

> ☆**WARNING** Different DOM implementations include different pieces as valid nodes, so be sure to read the documentation for a particular DOM to see which pieces of the XML document it recognizes as valid node types.

Table 8.1 Microsoft DOM Properties

Property Name	Description
`childNodes`	Lists child nodes for nodes with descendants
`documentElement`	The root node (root element) of the document
`firstChild`	The first child node of the current node
`lastChild`	The last child node of the current node
`nodeName`	The name of the node (element, attribute or entity name, for example)
`nodeValue`	The value, or content, of a node

Table 8.2 Microsoft DOM Methods

Method Name	Description
`Load()`	Loads an XML document
`GetElementsByTagName()`	Returns the elements that contain the specified name
`Clonenode()`	Makes a copy of the current node
`CreateNode()`	Creates a node
`CreateElement()`	Creates an element node
`CreateAttribute()`	Creates an attribute node
`CreateEntityReference()`	Creates an entity reference
`HasChildNodes()`	Will return a value of "true" if the current node has child nodes
`Save()`	Saves the document

Let's look at an example of how to use some of these properties and methods. In this example, you will create some JavaScript code inside an HTML page that uses Microsoft's DOM. Your program will read and process the Job Postings XML document from earlier in this chapter. Following is the HTML file that contains the JavaScript code. The comments explain each section. The syntax for the comment lines is defined on line 6.

```
<html>
<head>
<title>Microsoft DOM Example Using Javascript</title>
<body>
<script language="javascript">
/* This is a comment in JavaScript */
/* Create a new DOM object for our document */
var xmlDocument = new ActiveXObject("Microsoft.XMLDOM");
xmlDocument.async="false";
/* Use the "load" method to read our XML document into memory */
xmlDocument.load("job-posting.xml");
/* Print some HTML code */
document.write("<p><strong>Using the Microsoft DOM </strong></p>");
/* BEGIN THE EXAMPLES */
/* 1. Prints the value of the first child node */
document.write("<p>1. <strong>firstChild</strong> is: ");
document.write(xmlDocument.documentElement.firstChild.text);
document.write("</p>");
/* 2. Prints the value of the last child node */
document.write("<p>2. <strong>lastChild</strong> is: ");
document.write(xmlDocument.documentElement.lastChild.text);
document.write("</p>");
/* 3. Prints the name of the lastChild element */
document.write("<p>3. <strong>lastChild</strong> node name is: ");
document.write(xmlDocument.documentElement.lastChild.nodeName);
document.write("</p>");
/* 4. Prints the name of the child node stored in item(1) */
/* Then, it checks to see if the node has child elements */
document.write("<p>4. <strong>item(2)</strong> is: ");
document.write(xmlDocument.documentElement.childNodes.item(2).nodeName);
document.write("</p><p>  Does this node have child elements? ");
document.write(xmlDocument.documentElement.childNodes.item(2).hasChildNodes());
document.write("</p>");
/* End the examples */
</script>
</body>
</html>
```

☆ **TIP** The `item()` method contains the element numbers in order. When you use `item()` to locate a specific element, start counting elements at 0, not 1. So the first element in the list of elements would be `item(0)`—in this case, the `<description>` element.

Here are a few JavaScript tips:

- Each line in JavaScript ends with a semicolon (`;`).
- The `document.write()` function in JavaScript simply prints to the screen the value of what is contained in the parentheses. For example, the following line would print `"Hello"` to the screen:

  ```
  document.write("Hello");
  ```

- If you are accessing the components of an object—in this example, the `xmlDocument` object—you must preface each expression with this object name. An **expression** is a single piece of information within programming code. For example, on line 17 of the HTML file, you print the content of the first child element in the XML document:

  ```
  document.write(xmlDocument.documentElement.
  firstChild.text);
  ```

  Notice that the name of the object, `xmlDocument`, is the first piece of information in this expression. Each piece of the expression is separated by a period. The second piece, `documentElement`, tells the application that you're looking for an element. The third piece, `firstChild`, defines the desired element, and the last piece, `text`, says that you want the text, or content, of that element.

Figure 8.2 shows the HTML page in Internet Explorer. Notice that it has printed the values for each of the pieces of information you asked for in the JavaScript code.

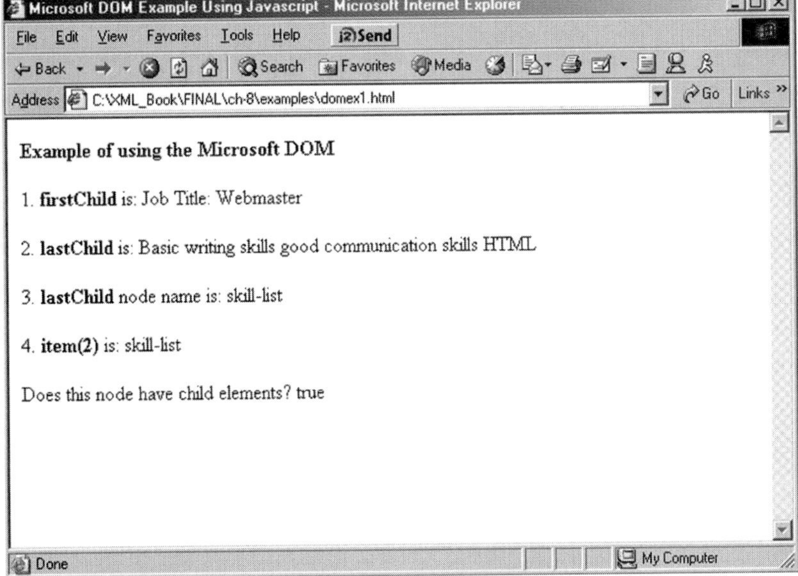

Figure 8.2 HTML Page with JavaScript Program for Accessing XML Data Using Microsoft's DOM

☆ **SHORTCUT** Try this example yourself. Here's how:

1. Create an XML file called `job-posting.xml` using the Job Postings XML file.
2. Create an HTML file called `example1.html` using the code shown here.
3. Save both files in the same directory on your hard drive.
4. Open the HTML file in Internet Explorer, version 5.0 or later.
5. Try changing some of the information in both the XML file and the JavaScript code to produce different results.

The Simple Application Programming Interface for XML

The Simple Application Programming Interface (API) for XML (SAX) provides another method of processing XML documents. The SAX 1.0 recommendation was released by the W3C in May 1998. SAX, like DOM, provides an interface to XML documents. But SAX does not produce a tree structure of nodes that represent the XML document. Instead, SAX is an **event-based** API, meaning that it reads an XML document, starting at the top, and creates various **events** that are passed to **event handlers** within the program. Because the document is read in a serial fashion, the program cannot jump around from node to node as in DOM. This type of processing makes SAX very fast, and it uses very little memory because it does not store the data.

Let's look at an example of how SAX works. Following is a small XML document:

```
<?xml version="1.0"?>
<book id="1234">
   <title>The Web Wizard's Guide to XML</title>
   <author>C. Hughes</author>
</book>
```

Following are the individual events that would be created by a SAX application processing the sample document:

```
1  Start document
2  Start element (book)
3  Attribute (id="1234")
4  Start element (title)
5  Text (The Web Wizard's Guide to XML)
6  End element (title)
7  Start element (author)
8  Text (C. Hughes)
9  End element (author)
10 End element (book)
11 End document
```

SAX is commonly used to search large documents for particular pieces of information. SAX also allows you to stop the processing once you have found what you are looking for. In contrast, DOM requires the entire document be loaded into memory before processing begins. The next section describes various scenarios and discusses whether SAX or DOM is the better tool for the job.

Comparing SAX and DOM

The choice of whether to use SAX, DOM, or a combination of the two depends largely on the program or task at hand. The next two sections cover scenarios for using SAX and DOM.

When to Use SAX

Because SAX is an event-driven API, it uses very little memory and is well suited for certain tasks in which you don't need the overhead of DOM. Following are a few situations when SAX would be the better choice.

- Processing large documents: If you need to process very large documents, the amount of memory required to create the DOM tree structure may be too large for the resources to handle. Using SAX can speed the process and also save on memory utilization because SAX does not store the document pieces in memory. This solution works best if the document is only meant to be read, not modified.
- Searching: If you are performing a search function, it is usually not necessary to store the entire document in memory; you simply want to look through the file for certain information and then process the information. SAX is a good choice for this type of task because it can quickly read through the document and return the desired information to an event handler for processing. Because SAX does not require the extra processing resources to store data to memory, it is much faster than DOM.
- Stopping the program: For certain tasks, after you have found what you are looking for there is no need to continue processing the XML document. SAX allows you to stop the program at any time, thereby saving resources by not performing unnecessary processing. This functionality comes in handy when you're doing searches. After you have found what you are looking for, you can stop the process. Using DOM, you must first read the entire document into memory and then search for the desired information.

When to Use DOM

Many programs and tasks call for modifying or manipulating the XML document. This is a task that DOM is better suited for. Following are a few situations when DOM would be the better choice.

- Accessing cross-referenced data: For this kind of data, DOM is the better choice. Because SAX processes the file from the top down, it is impossible to go back up through the document. DOM comes in handy, for example, when a node needs to access data from a parent or sibling node.
- Modifying an XML document: If you need to modify the pieces of an XML document during processing, DOM can handle this because it has the information stored in memory. Using DOM, you can modify the information and then save the changes.
- Creating new XML documents: SAX cannot be used to create new documents. DOM allows you to create new XML documents or XML documents based on information obtained from other XML documents.

XML and Programming Languages

Because of its structure, XML has become a popular language to use in combination with object-oriented programming languages. The DOM model provides a perfect interface to application objects that are created in programs. Java, Perl, and C++ are currently the most popular object-oriented languages used for Web applications.

Sun Microsystems, creator of Java, has embraced XML and provides a variety of APIs and architectures using XML and Java together. Examples are Java Architecture for XML Binding (JAXB), Java API for XML Messaging (JAXM), and Java API for XML Processing (JAXP). XML is also being used in enterprise Java application development environments, such as IBM's WebSphere Suite and Sun's Netscape Application Server. Both are Java application servers that have extensive built-in support for XML.

The Perl programming language also provides a number of modules for working with XML, including XML::Parser, XML::DOM, and XML::Grove. Perl's primary strength lies in text manipulation, and it provides several modules for creating XML documents from data stored in other formats, such as databases, spreadsheets, and delimited files (such as a CSV—comma separated value—file).

XML and Databases

The structured nature of XML makes it a perfect technology for storing data. The choice of whether to use XML or a relational database, such as Access or Oracle, largely depends on the requirements of the program or project.

Databases store data in a structured way, using tables and fields—as opposed to named elements—to label the information. XML can be used like a database but can also support relationships that are not easily represented in a database. For example, XML provides the element hierarchy—siblings, descendants, ancestors—and information about the relationships between and among elements. This kind of storage is difficult for a relational database because the tables and fields are not structured in this manner.

XML is becoming the format of choice for storing data because it is cross-platform and vendor-independent, but databases still offer greater speed and flexibility in accessing the information. XML has proven to be useful for projects in which many kinds of data sources and programs must work together. XML also provides a common framework that supports various programs running on various platforms.

WARNING Even though XML is powerful, it may not be the right tool to use for every project, especially those with large amounts of data that must be manipulated. For some programs, the speed and querying power of a relational database may be a better solution. Be sure to analyze all your options to make sure that you choose the right tools for the job. Remember, though, that many of the large database vendors support XML and allow you to import and export data as XML files.

XML Query Language (XQuery)

The XQuery specification is still in draft format and has not yet been released as a recommendation by the W3C. A Working Draft was released in December 2001. The specification is being developed as a query language that will span all types of XML documents and data sources. The goal of XQuery is to provide a standard language that can be used for querying XML documents and databases.

At this point, XQuery does not have many working programs because it has not been finalized. Many developers are using other technologies, such as DOM, to perform queries. Or they import the XML data into a relational database, process it, and then export the results in XML format. In "Online References" at the end of the chapter you can find more information about XQuery and its current status.

TIP Keep an eye on the progress of the XQuery specification on the W3C's Web site. This technology has a lot of support from large database vendors and is poised to play an important role in the future of database programming.

A Sampling of XML Programs

Many XML vocabularies have already been written, and some are being developed as standards within specific industries. For example, the Wireless Application Protocol (WAP) is an XML vocabulary that is becoming the standard for marking up content being sent to and read via wireless devices such as cell phones. This section reviews a few of the XML vocabularies that are available or in the process of being developed.

Distributed Authoring and Versioning on the World Wide Web (WebDAV)

`http://www.webdav.org`

WebDAV is being developed as a proposed standard for distributed Web authoring. It is a set of methods that extend the Hypertext Transfer Protocol (HTTP) to allow users to edit, view, search, delete, and manage files on a remote Web server. This will allow teams of developers to work together from different locations.

Wireless Application Protocol (WAP)

http://www.wapforum.org

The WAP Forum Web site defines WAP as "an open, global specification that empowers mobile users with wireless devices to easily access and interact with information and services instantly." WAP is being developed as the standard markup language for viewing content on wireless devices, much as HTML was developed as the standard for viewing content on the Web. Many leaders in the wireless communications industry are part of this group, including Motorola, IBM, and Ericsson. The WAP Forum is currently working with the W3C to develop a formal recommendation for WAP.

Scalable Vector Graphics (SVG)

http://www.w3c.org/Graphics/SVG

SVG version 1.0 was released as a recommendation by the W3C in September 2001. SVG is being developed as the standard for describing graphical content in XML. These two-dimensional graphics consist of vector graphics (straight lines and curves), images, and text. SVG graphics can be interactive and dynamic and can be further enhanced by using a scripting language.

Open Financial Exchange (OFX)

http://www.ofx.net

OFX is a specification for exchanging financial data among financial institutions, businesses, and consumers via the Internet. It was developed by CheckFree, Intuit, and Microsoft in 1997 as a way for financial institutions to exchange information. OFX was not originally written in XML but became XML 1.0–compliant with the version 2.0 release in 2000. According to the OFX Web site, OFX "supports a wide range of financial activities including consumer and small business banking, consumer and small business bill payment, bill presentment, and investments tracking, including stocks, bonds, mutual funds, and 401(k) account details."

Mathematical Markup Language (MathML)

http://www.w3c.org/Math

MathML was one of the first XML languages. The W3C released the version 2.0 recommendation in February 2001. MathML is an XML vocabulary used to describe mathematical notations. The next section presents examples.

Chemical Markup Language (CML)

http://www.xml-cml.org

CML was developed as a means of describing complex chemical equations and molecular information, including organic molecules, quantum chemistry, and inorganic crystallography. CML has interfaces to various programming languages, including Java, C++, and Corba.

Extensible Hypertext Markup Language (XHTML)

http://www.w3c.org/TR/xhtml1

XHTML, version 1.0, was released as a recommendation by the W3C in January 2000 as a transition language between HTML and XML. In Chapter One, you learned a little bit about XHTML and ways it is being used.

Resource Description Framework (RDF)

http://www.w3c.org/RDF

Released as a recommendation by the W3C in February 1999, RDF was developed as a framework for processing metadata to provide interoperability between programs that exchange information on the Web. This information is meant to be understood by machines and not necessarily by people. RDF can be used to provide better search engine capabilities, to describe content relationships, and to catalog information.

An Example: MathML

Let's look at an example of how to use MathML to mark up a few equations. Tables 8.3 and 8.4 list a few of the MathML elements and entities as defined in the MathML 2.0 specification.

Table 8.3 Selected MathML Elements

Element Name	Description
`mi`	Identifier for a variable name, constant, or function name
`mo`	Operator or separator
`mn`	A number
`mtext`	Text
`mspace`	A space character
`mrow`	Horizontal group of any number of subexpressions
`mfrac`	Form a fraction from two subexpressions
`mfenced`	Surround content with a pair of "fences," such as parentheses (the default), brackets, or braces
`plus`	Addition (empty element)
`minus`	Subtraction (empty element)
`over`	Division (empty element)

(continues)

Table 8.3 Selected MathML Elements *(continued)*

Element Name	Description
`times`	Multiplication (empty element)
`apply`	Used to group operators with elements
`ci`	Content identifier
`cn`	Content number

Table 8.4 Selected MathML Entities

Entity Name	Description
`<`	Less than
`>`	Greater than
`⁢`	Represents an implied multiplication (can also use ⁢)
`⁡`	Used for mathematical functions (can also use ⁡)

Following are examples of mathematical equations and their corresponding MathML representations.

$3 + 5$

```
1 <mrow>
2   <mn> 3 </mn>
3   <mo> + </mo>
4   <mn> 5 </mn>
5 </mrow>
```

Lines 1 and 5 start and end the group. Lines 2 and 4 contain the numbers being summed (3 and 5). Line 3 contains the + addition operator.

$(x + y)$

```
<mrow>
  <mo> ( </mo)
  <mrow>
      <mi> x </mi>
      <mo> + </mo>
      <mi> y </mi>
  </mrow>
  <mo> ) </mo>
</mrow>
```

Lines 1 and 9 start and end the outermost group. Lines 2 and 8 contain the open and close parentheses. Lines 4 and 6 contain the names of the variables **x** and **y**. Notice that the <mi> element is used in this example (instead of the <mn> element from the first example) because you are using variables instead of actual numbers on lines 4 and 6. Line 5 contains the + addition operator. The inner equation is contained within a nested <mrow> element.

ab

```
1 <mrow>
2   <mi> x </mi>
3   <mo> &InvisibleTimes; </mo>
4   <mi> b </mi>
5 </mrow>
```

Lines 1 and 5 start and end the group. Lines 2 and 4 contain the names of the variables a and b. Line 3 contains the entity name `⁢` to indicate that these two variables should be multiplied but that no operator character should be displayed.

$\sin x$

```
1 <mrow>
2   <mi> sin </mi>
3   <mo> &ApplyFunction; </mo>
4   <mi> x </mi>
5 </mrow>
```

Lines 1 and 5 start and end the group. Line 2 contains the function name `sin`. Line 3 contains the entity name `⁡`, which tells the parser to apply the `sin` function to the variable `x` on line 4.

$2 + 3x + 5 = 0$

```
<mrow>
    <mrow>
        <mn> 2 </mn>
        <mo> + </mo>
        <mrow>
            <mn> 3 </mn>
            <mo> &InvisibleTimes; </mo>
            <mi> x </mi>
        </mrow>
        <mo> + </mo>
        <mn> 5 </mn>
    </mrow>
    <mo> = </mo>
    <mn> 0 </mn>
</mrow>
```

An Example: MathML

Lines 1 and 15 start and end the outermost group. This example contains two nested <mrow> elements: one that begins on line 2 and ends on line 12, and another that begins on line 5 and ends on line 9.

(a + 2) * b

```
1 <mrow>
2     <apply>
3        <times/>
4        <apply>
5             <plus/>
6             <ci>a</ci>
7             <cn>2</cn>
8        </apply>
9        <ci>b</ci>
10    </apply>
11 </mrow>
```

This example uses the <apply> element to express the equation. The first <apply> element on line 2 opens the multiplication expression. The order of the elements is important. The first item in this expression is `(a + 2)`, and the second is `b`. The nested <apply> expression starts on line 4 and ends on line 8. It "applies" the <plus/> element on line 5 to add the two content elements on lines 6 and 7. Like the <mi> and <mn> elements from the earlier examples, the <ci> element is used to mark up the variables on lines 6 and 9, and the <cn> element is used to mark up the number on line 7.

The Future of XML

Because XML is a new technology, it will take some time to reach its full potential. Many components of XML are still in the beginning stages of development. Sources within the industry see XML as the future of the Web, especially for e-commerce applications, and they expect the usefulness of the Web to increase exponentially because of the power of XML. Programs that process XML will become increasingly powerful as new technologies, such as XSL and XML Schema, mature.

For XML to become the standard technology for exchanging and storing data, it must be accepted by industry leaders, something that is already happening. The vocabularies you learned about earlier in this chapter have the support of industry giants such as IBM, Microsoft, and Motorola. If the phenomenal success of HTML over the past decade is any indication of the value of a cross-platform, vendor-independent document format, then the possibilities for XML are endless.

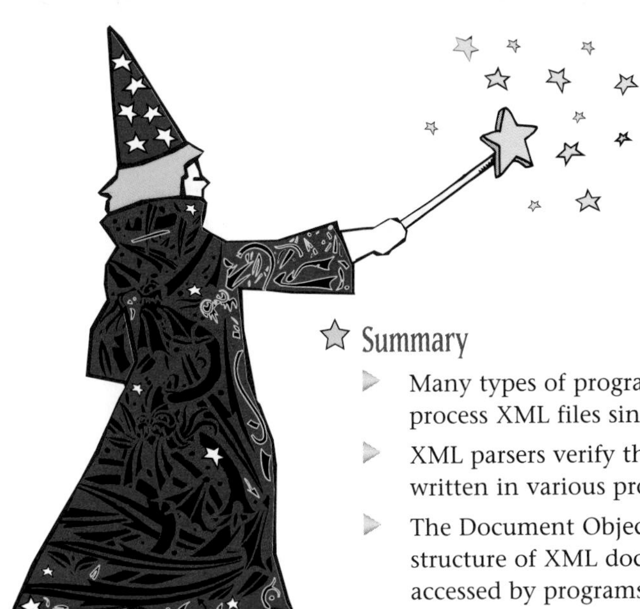

Summary

- Many types of programs have been developed to use and process XML files since XML was first developed.
- XML parsers verify the syntax of XML documents and are written in various programming languages.
- The Document Object Model (DOM) in XML creates a tree structure of XML documents in memory that can then be accessed by programs. DOM is easily compatible with object-oriented programming languages. DOM methods and properties can be used to access certain nodes in the document tree.
- SAX is an event-based programming interface for XML files. SAX does not store the XML document in memory; as a result, it uses very little memory and is very fast.
- The decision of whether to use SAX or DOM to process your XML documents depends on the needs of your application.
- XML has extensive support for object-oriented programming languages such as C++, Java, and Perl.
- XML is becoming the method of choice for storing data. The XML Query Language (XQuery) provides a querying language for XML documents.
- A wide variety of XML mark-up languages are available today, including languages for web development, wireless application development and standards within certain industries such as financial or scientific.
- One XML-based language, MathML, is being used as the standard language to mark-up mathematical documents and formulas.
- XML appears to be well on its way to widespread acceptance as the standard language for document types that need to be shared among many companies or many users.

Online References

W3C's DOM Site
`http://www.w3.org/DOM`

W3C: DOM Level 1 Specification
`http://www.w3.org/TR/REC-DOM-Level-1/`

W3C: DOM Level 2 Core Specification
`http://www.w3.org/TR/2000/REC-DOM-Level-2-Core-20001113`

W3C: DOM Level 2 HTML Specification
`http://www.w3.org/TR/2000/WD-DOM-Level-2-HTML-20001113/`

W3C: DOM Level 3 Specification
`http://www.w3.org/TR/2002/WD-DOM-Level-3-Core-20020114`

W3C: XQuery Specification
`http://www.w3.org/TR/xquery/`

The Java Language and XML
`http://java.sun.com/xml/`

W3C: MathML Fundamentals
`http://www.w3.org/TR/MathML2/chapter2.html`

XML: Proposed Applications and Industry Initiatives
`http://www.oasis-open.org/cover/xml.html#applications`

XML, the Future of the Web
`http://www.acm.org/crossroads/xrds6-2/future.html`

☆Review Questions

1. What is the purpose of an XML parser?
2. List two differences between DOM and SAX.
3. Describe a program that would benefit from DOM over SAX.
4. Describe a program that would benefit from SAX over DOM.
5. What do XML files have in common with databases?
6. What is one advantage of XML over databases for preserving data relationships?
7. Which XML language is being used for developing wireless applications?
8. List a few reasons that an industry, such as the financial industry, would want to develop a common language using XML.

☆Hands-On Exercises

1. Using the Microsoft DOM described in this chapter, describe the data being accessed by the following:

   ```
   xmlDocument.documentElement.firstChild.nodeName
   ```

2. Using the following XML document, what is the value of the expression in Exercise 1?

   ```
   <?xml version="1.0"?>
   <meeting_notes>
        <topic>Holiday Parth</topic>
        <date>August 23, 2001</date>
        <agenda>
              <item>Location</item>
              <item>Date</item>
              <item>Menu</item>
              <item>Entertainment</item>
        </agenda>
   </meeting_notes>
   ```

3. Using the JavaScript example from earlier in the chapter, create the code to output the name and content contained in the <date> element.
4. Create the XML file from Exercise 2. Create an HTML page with JavaScript code, as in the example earlier in this chapter, that prints the node names and values for each of the elements in the XML document you just created.
5. Create the MathML markup for the following two equations:

   a. `3+4+n`

   b. `2x+6=7y`

APPENDIX A: XML TOOLS AND RESOURCES

Hundreds of XML tools are available to help you develop XML documents and programs. This appendix contains a small subset to get you started. Many of these tools are free to use for personal development or for nonprofit organizations. Some require a licensing fee if the tools are to be used for commercial purposes; please refer to the respective Web sites for information about pricing. The information provided here was gathered from documentation obtained on the Web, and although every effort has been made to verify the information, it is not guaranteed to be accurate.

XML Browsers

Internet Explorer

- Vendor: Microsoft Corporation
- URL: `http://www.microsoft.com/windows/ie/default.asp`

Netscape 6

- Vendor: Netscape Communications Corporation
- URL: `http://home.netscape.com/computing/download/index.html`

Opera

- Vendor: Opera Software
- URL: `http://www.opera.com`

XML Parsers

Xerces

- Vendor: The Apache XML Project
- URL (Java 2.0 parser): `http://xml.apache.org/xerces2-j/index.html`
- URL (C++ parser): `http://xml.apache.org/xerces-c/index.html`
- URL (Perl parser): `http://xml.apache.org/xerces-p/index.html`
- Description from the vendor Web site: "Xerces (named after the Xerces Blue butterfly) provides world-class XML parsing and generation. Fully-validating

parsers are available for both Java and C++, implementing the W3C XML and DOM (Level 1 and 2) standards, as well as the de facto SAX (version 2) standard. The parsers are highly modular and configurable. Initial support for XML Schema (draft W3C standard) is also provided."

MSXML 4.0

- Vendor: Microsoft Corporation
- URL: `http://msdn.microsoft.com/downloads/default.asp?url=/downloads/topic.asp?URL=/MSDN-FILES/028/000/072/topic.xml`
- Description from the vendor Web site: "Support of the World Wide Web (W3) Consortium final recommendation for XML Schema, with both DOM and SAX. New and substantially faster SAX parser. Better support for sequential architectures and streamed XML processing based on SAX 2, including DOM-SAX integration and HTML generation. Improved standards conformance and scalability."

Expat—XML Parser Toolkit

- Vendor: Thai Open Source Software Center Ltd.
- URL: `http://www.jclark.com/xml/expat.html`
- Description from the vendor Web site: "Expat is an XML 1.0 parser written in C. It aims to be fully conforming. It is currently not a validating XML processor."

XML Parser for Java

- Vendor: IBM AlphaWorks
- URL: `http://www.alphaworks.ibm.com/tech/xml4j`
- Description from the vendor Web site: "XML Parser for Java is a validating XML parser and processor written in 100% pure Java; it is a library for parsing and generating XML documents. This parser easily enables an application to read and write XML data."

XML Editors

Xeena

- Vendor: IBM AlphaWorks
- URL: `http://www.alphaworks.ibm.com/tech/xeena`
- Description from the vendor Web site: "Xeena, a visual XML editor, is a generic Java application for editing valid XML documents derived from any

valid DTD. XML files can be created and edited without learning the intricacies of XML. The editor takes as input a given DTD and automatically builds a palette containing the elements defined in the DTD. Any document derived from that DTD by using a visual, tree-directed paradigm can thus be created, edited, or expanded. The visual paradigm requires only a minimal learning curve, because only valid constructs or elements are presented to the user in a context-sensitive palette."

XML Spy Document Editor

- Vendor: Altova, Inc.
- URL: `http://www.xmlspy.com`
- Description from the vendor Web site: "XML Spy Document Editor empowers non-technical people to easily create and edit XML content through a user interface that closely resembles an easy-to-use word-processor."

XMetaL

- Vendor: Corel Corporation
- URL: `http://www.softquad.com/top_frame.sq`
- Description from the vendor Web site: "XMetaL is a full-featured validating XML editor that supports all the advanced constructs necessary to create both valid and well formed XML. These core features and capabilities provide the foundation for building intuitive XML content editing applications. XMetaL 3 breaks new ground by supporting significant document editing features of W3C Schema (XSD) for rich content validation. Providing unprecedented flexibility, XMetaL will load either a W3C Schema or a DTD, to allow organizations to develop with whichever schema language best suit their needs."

XML Notepad

- Vendor: Microsoft Corporation
- URL: `http://msdn.microsoft.com/xml/notepad/intro.asp`
- Description from the vendor Web site: "Microsoft XML Notepad is a simple prototyping application for HTML authors and developers that enables the rapid building and editing of small sets of XML-based data. With XML Notepad, developers can quickly create XML prototypes in an iterative fashion, using familiar metaphors. XML Notepad offers an intuitive and simple user interface that graphically represents the tree structure of XML data. Working with the standard building blocks of XML supported in Microsoft Internet Explorer 4.0, authors are able to create reproducible data structures that can be easily filled, allowing greater emphasis to be placed on application development instead of manual data structuring."

XML Application Development

XMI Toolkit

- Vendor: IBM AlphaWorks
- URL: `http://www.alphaworks.ibm.com/tech/xmitoolkit`
- Description from the vendor Web site: "XMI Toolkit is a Java component that allows sharing of Java objects using XML, generation of DTDs, and conversion of designs and code between Java, UML, and Rational Rose."

XML Spy Suite

- Vendor: Altova, Inc.
- URL: `http://www.xmlspy.com`
- Description from the vendor Web site: "XML Spy 4.3 Suite now includes an innovative XML Spy 4.3 XSLT Designer that automates the generation of XSLT Stylesheets, and the XML Spy 4.3 Document Editor that empowers non-technical people to easily create and edit XML content through a user interface that closely resembles an easy-to-use word-processor."

Java Web Services Developer Pack

- Vendor: Sun Microsystems, Inc.
- URL:
  `http://java.sun.com/webservices/webservicespack.html`
- Description from the vendor Web site: "The Java Web Services Developer Pack (Java WSDP) is an all-in-one download containing key technologies to simplify building of web services using the Java 2 Platform."

Oracle XML Developer's Kit

- Vendor: Oracle Corporation
- URL: `http://otn.oracle.com/tech/xml/xdkhome.html`
- Description from the vendor Web site: "The Oracle XML Developer's Kits (XDK) contain the basic building blocks for reading, manipulating, transforming and viewing XML documents. To provide a broad variety of deployment options, the Oracle XDKs are available for Java, JavaBeans, C, C++ and PL/SQL. Unlike many shareware and trial XML components, the production Oracle XDKs are fully supported and come with a commercial redistribution license."

APPENDIX B: ANSWERS TO ODD-NUMBERED REVIEW QUESTIONS

Chapter One

1. A markup language is a set of rules that define the layout, format, or structure of text within a document. The language consists of syntax rules and instructions that tell applications how to process the document
3. Some limitations of HTML are: the set of elements that can be used is finite and cannot be extended; HTML elements describe format, not data; and HTML documents are difficult to search.
5. The starting tag, content, and the ending tag
7. Three differences between HTML and XML are:
   1. XML is not dependent on a single document type like HTML.
   2. XML allows you to define your own elements; HTML does not.
   3. XML element names are case-sensitive; HTML elements are not.
9. You would convert HTML documents to XHTML documents if you wanted to use the documents with an XML processing program. XHTML is XML-compliant, while HTML is not. You may also convert your documents from HTML to XHTML as a first step in transitioning to XML.

Chapter Two

1. It is important to adhere to the syntax rules for XML to ensure that your documents make sense to other people and applications that use your XML documents.
3. Element nesting refers to containing elements within other elements. Elements are nested to provide relationships among and between different elements.
5. Attributes are used to provide descriptive information about elements, much like adjectives and adverbs do in the English language. They are always located within the start tag of the element.
7. Internal content entities are defined inside the XML document itself; external entities are defined in separate files and are read when the document is processed.

Chapter Three

1. Syntax refers to the rules for creating the components of the document, and structure refers to how those components fit together and relate to each other.
3. The `standalone` attribute in the XML declaration tells the processing application that everything needed to process the document is contained within the XML document, and that no external files should be read in at the time of processing.
5. The + character notation means that one or more occurrences of the element are required.
7. The internal DTD would take precedence.
9. Two advantages of XML schemas over DTDs are:
   1. XML schemas are written using XML syntax; DTDs are not.
   2. XML schemas provide more data types than DTDs.

Chapter Four

1. A few benefits of separating content from style are: It allows you to describe the data, not the format; many different formats can be created for a single document by creating multiple style sheets; and a single style sheet can be used to provide formatting information for many XML documents.
3. To apply a single CSS style sheet to many different documents, simply create a style sheet that contains all of the styles necessary for all of the documents you wish to format, and then reference this style sheet in the declaration line of all of the XML documents. This way, if you need to change a particular style on all of the documents, you just need to change it in the style sheet.
5. You would use a default rule declaration in the style sheet.
7. Two weaknesses of CSS are:
   1. CSS does not use the XML syntax.
   2. CSS cannot perform computations or make logical decisions based on the content.

Chapter Five

1. Namespaces in XML are used to prevent confusion if element names represent two different meanings within a single document. This is very important when different XML document types are merged together.
3. One way to correct a naming collision is to create one prefixed namespace for one of the document types. A second way would be to create separate name-

spaces for each document type to identify which elements belong to which document type—these namespaces could be either default or prefixed depending on the structure of the documents.

5. Two types of URIs used to identify namespaces are URL (Uniform Resource Locator) and URN (Uniform Resource Name).
7. Yes, default and prefixed namespaces can be used within the same document.
9. No, the element on which the namespace is declared does not have to belong to that namespace. It can belong to a different namespace or to no namespace at all.

Chapter Six

1. Simple XLink links only all for unidirectional links to a single target resource. Extended XLink links are much more powerful, and allow for multi-directional links to multiple target resources, among other more powerful features.
3. Any XML element can be a link.
5. The five possible values of the `show` attribute are `replace`, `new`, `embed`, `other`, and `none`.
7. The `five` possible values that can be assigned to the type attribute for extended links are `extended`, `resource`, `locator`, `arc`, and `title`.

Chapter Seven

1. The namespace for XSLT is `http://www.w3.org/1999/XSL/Transform`
3. The component of XSL that defined formatting properties is XSL-FO.
5. The for-each loop within an XSL template tells the processor to iterate over each instance of the object being searched for and perform a set of functions on each instance. For example, a for-each loop could be used to look for all instances of a particular element within a document and then format each instance in a certain way.
7. Three XML schema built-in datatypes are: integer, date, string.
9. The difference between simple and complex XSL schema types is that simple types can only define an element that has no attributes or child elements.

Chapter Eight

1. An XML parser is used to check the syntax and, if it is a validating parser, the content model of an XML document. The parser will report errors if the document does not adhere.

3. A program that would benefit from DOM over SAX would be a program that needed to access cross-referenced data or that needed to access data about an element's parent element.

5. XML files and databases both define the structure and data of content by placing labels on the content—databases use tables and fields, and XML uses elements.

7. XML can preserve data relationships because of the inheritance structure of elements within an XML document. Using inheritance, elements can be grouped together, for example, in a parent-child or sibling relationship. These relationships among elements are difficult to replicate in a database because of the nature of how databases store data.

INDEX

A

<a> Anchor element, HTML, 100–103
Absolute URLs, 102
Acrole attribute, 107–109
Actuate attribute, 106–107
Anchor <a> element, HTML, 100–103
Attributes
  acrole, 107–109
  actuate, 106–107
  attribute group, 62
  defined, 23–24
  DTD, 54–58
  href, 106
  role, 107–109
  show, 106–107
  simple links, 106–109
  standalone, 49
  title, 107–109
  type, 106
  well-formed documents and, 33
Authoring, 145
Authoring HTML Basics Web site, 17

B

Binary format, 4
Boilerplate documents, 26
Bolding text, 2–3, 8–9
Border properties, 72–73
Browser XML Display Chart online, 17
Browsers. *See* Web browsers

C

C++ compilers, 35
Cascading Style Sheets. *See* CSS (Cascading Style Sheets)
Case-sensitivity
  DOCUTYPE, 50
  well-formed documents, 34
  XML vs. HTML, 11
CERN (European Organization for Nuclear Research), 5, 17
Character entities, 25–26
Character notations, 54
Chemical Markup Language (CML), 146
Child and parent elements, 14, 22, 33
Client programs, 6
CML (Chemical Markup Language), 146
Code, defined, 2
Collapsed elements, 15
Color properties, 71–72
Compilers, 35
Complex type schema elements, 130–131
Constraints, occurrence, 128
Content developers, 4
Content entities, 26–27
Content model, DTD element declarations, 50–53
Content tags, 21
Content vs. design, 10–11, 13, 68
Content vs. presentation. *See* presentation
Conversion programs, 4
CSS (Cascading Style Sheets)
  comments, 70
  default values, 76–77
  exercises, 81–82
  online references, 80–81
  overview, 68–69
  property inheritance, 77–78
  pros and cons, 78–79
  review questions, 81
  rules syntax, 69
  style sheets, 69
  syntax and properties, 69–73

D

Data
  datatype attributes and, 55
  hierarchy of, 14–16
  presentation vs., 10–11, 13, 68
  XML datatypes, 128
Databases, 144–145
Decimal values, character entities, 26
Declarations
  CSS and, 69
  defined, 20–21
  DOCUTYPE, 49–50
  DTD element, 49–54
  external entity declarations, 30–31
  namespace, 86–88, 90–91
  parsed document with entity declarations, 28–29
Default namespaces, 87, 90–91
Default values
  attributes, 55
  CSS, 76–77
  namespaces, 87, 90–91
Design vs. content, 10–11, 13, 68
Display properties, 73
Distributed Authoring and Versioning on the Web (WebDAV), 145

Document components
attributes, 23–24
declarations, 20–21
DTD. *see* DTD (document type definition)
elements, 21–23
entities, 24–32
Document, defined, 8
Document models
DTDs, 42–43
schemas, 42–43
validating parsers, 44–48
DOCUTYPE, 49–50
DOM (Document Object Model)
defined, 137
Microsoft's XMLDOM, 138–142
online references, 151–152
SAX, 143–144
DTD (document type definition)
attributes, 54–58
character notations, 54
content model, 50–53
defined, 42–43
element declarations, 49–54
exercises, 64–65
extended links, 112–113
external, 49, 59–61
internal, 27, 49–58, 61
online references, 63
overview, 48–49
parsers, 44–48
public, 61
review questions, 64
schemas, 61–63
simple links, 109–111
summary, 62

E

E-mail messages, 50–53, 56–58
Elements
<a> anchor, 100–103
DTD element declarations, 49–54
empty, 23
HTML, 6–9, 100–103
<img> image, 103
legal and illegal names, 35
nesting, 14, 22
parent and child, 14, 22, 33
root, 14–16, 22
sibling, 22
tags, 21
XML, 10, 14
Empty elements, 23
End tags, 21
Entities
character, 25–26
content, 25
defined, 24
general, 25
unparsed, 25, 32
Error messages, 25–26, 45–48
European Organization for Nuclear Research (CERN), 5, 17
Event-based API, 142–143
Event handlers, 142
Events, 142
Extended links, 111–113
Extensibility, 5
Extensible Hypertext Markup Language (XHTML), 12, 147
Extensible Style Sheet Language (XSL). *See* XSL (Extensible Style Sheet Language)
External DTDs, 49, 59–61
External entities, 27, 30–31

F

Font properties, 70–71
FOP (Formatting Objects Processor), 119
Formatting properties, CSS, 70–73
Formatting template, 123–125

G

General entities, 25

H

Hierarchy, XML data, 14–16
Href attribute, 106
HTML
<a> anchor element, 100–103
Authoring HTML Basics Web site, 17
case-sensitivity, 11
content developers, 4
elements, 6–9, 100–103
extensibility, 5
history of markup languages, 6–9
HTMLpage with JavaScript, 139–141
<img> image element, 103
links, 100–104
transforming to XML using style sheets, 122–127
XHTML, 12, 147
XML, 11–12, 122–127
HTML 4, 12, 147
Hyperlinks, 100–103

I

IANA (Internet Assigned Numbers Authority), 36
<img> Image element, HTML, 103
Instance documents, 127
Internal DTD declarations, 49–58, 61
Internal entities, 27–28
Internal subset of DTD, 27
International Organization for Standardization (ISO), 4, 17, 63
Internet Assigned Numbers Authority (IANA), 36
Internet Explorer
CSS, 69
error messages, 25–26

external entity
declarations, 30–31
HTMLpage with JavaScript
Program for Accessing
XML Data using
Microsoft's DOM,
139–141
namespaces, 92
parsed document with
entity declarations,
28–29
parsers, 44–45, 48, 53, 58
viewing documents
formatted with HTML
elements, 6–9
XML documents, viewing,
14
XML documents, with
style sheets, 75
XML documents, without
style sheet, 122
XML file formatted with
XSL style sheet, 126
XMLDOM, 138–142
Internet Explorer 4, 12
ISO (International
Organization for
Standardization), 4, 17,
63

J

Java
compilers, 35
JavaScript code, 139–141
online references, 152

L

Links
<a> anchor element,
100–103
absolute vs. relative URLs,
102
defined, 100
exercises, 115–116
extended, 111–113
HTML, 100–104
<img> image element, 103
online references, 114–115
overview, 99
review questions, 115
simple, 104–111
summary, 114
XML, 104
Looping, 123–124

M

MacIntosh, 2, 4, 8
Markup languages
fundamentals of, 2–4
HTML, 6–9
SGML, 4–6
MathML (Mathematical
Markup Language)
defined, 2
online references, 146–150
W3C Math ML
Fundamentals, 152
Metalanguage, defined, 2
Methods, DOM, 139
Microsoft
validating parsers, 44–47,
53, 63
XML web site, 17
XMLDOM, 138–142
Microsoft Word
bolding text, 2–3
proprietary format, 4
Multidirectional links, 104

N

Name-value pairs, 23–24
Named character entities, 26
Namespaces
avoiding confusion, 85–86
declarations, 86–88
defined, 84
exercises, 96–97
need for, 84–85
online references, 95
overview, 83
review questions, 96
scope of, 89–92
summary, 95
syntax, 86–89
URIs, 88–89
using, 92–94
XML instance document,
128
XML schema document,
127–128
XSL-FO, 119
XSLT Formatting Objects,
120
Naming collision, 85
Nesting, 14, 22, 33
Netscape Navigator, 4
Netscape Navigator 4, 12, 69
Netscape Navigator 6, 104
Nodes, 137
Nonvalidating parsers, 35,
44
Notepad, 8

O

Occurrence constraints, 128
OFX (Open Financial
Exchange), 146
Online references
CSS, 80–81
DOM, 151–152
DTD, 63
IANA, 36
International Character
Set, 36
Java and XML, 152
links, 114–115
MathML, 152
programming with XML,
151–152
schemas, 63, 132
style sheets, CSS, 80
style sheets, XSL, 132
Unicode, 36
validating parsers,
Microsoft, 44
W3C XML Specifications,
36
well-formed XML
documents, 36
XML specifications, 17, 18
XSL, 80
Open Financial Exchange
(OFX), 146
Overlapping, 33

P

Page, defined, 8
Parent and child elements, 14, 22, 33
Parsed document with entity declarations, 28–29
Parsers
  programming with XML, 136
  spaces, 51
  syntax, 35
Pattern matching, 125
PDAs (personal digital assistants), 6
PDFs (Portable Document Format) files, 68
Portability of documents, 4
Prefixed namespace declarations, 87–88, 91
Presentation
  content vs., 10–11, 13, 68
  CSS, using. *see* CSS (Cascading Style Sheets)
  overview, 67
Programming, with XML
  CML (Chemical Markup Language), 146
  databases, 144–145
  DOM, 137–142
  exercises, 152
  MathML, 146–150
  OFX (Open Financial Exchange), 146
  online references, 151–152
  overview, 136
  parsers, 136
  programming languages, 144
  RDF (Resource Description Framework), 147
  review questions, 152
  SAX, 142–144
  summary, 151
  SVG (Scalable Vector Graphics), 146
WAP (Wireless Application Protocol), 146
  WebDAV (Distributed Authoring and Versioning on the Web), 145
  XHTML, 147
Properties
  border, 72–73
  color, 71–72
  CSS, 69–73
  display, 73
  DOM, 139
  font, 70–71
  text, 71
Property inheritance, 77–78
Proprietary format, 4
Public DTDs, 61

Q

Query Language, XML (XQuery), 144–145

R

RDF (Resource Description Framework), 147
Reading documents, defined, 2
Relative URLs, 102
Resource Description Framework (RDF), 147
Role attribute, 107–109
Root elements, 14–16, 22
Root nodes, 137
Root tree, 120
Rule syntax, 69

S

SAX (API Simple Application Programming Interface for XML), 142–144
Scalable Vector Graphics (SVG), 146
Schemas
  datatypes, 128
  document models, 42–43
  exercises, 133–134
  importance of, 118
  occurrence constraints, 128
  online references, 132
  overview, 61–63, 117
  review questions, 133
  simple vs. complex elements, 129–131
  summary, 132
  syntax, 129–131
Scope, namespaces, 89–92
SGML (Standard Generalized Markup Language), 4–6, 9
Show attribute, 106–107
Sibling elements, 22
Simple Application Programming Interface for XML (SAX), 142–144
Simple links
  attributes, 106–109
  defined, 104–106
  defining in DTDs, 109–111
Simple type schema elements, 129
Source documents, 102
Source tree, 120
Standalone attribute, 49
Standard Generalized Markup Language (SGML), 4–6, 9
Start tags, 21
Strings, 34
Structured documents, 42–43
Style sheets
  CSS. *see* CSS (Cascading Style Sheets)
  data vs. presentation, 10–11, 13, 68
  XSL. *see* XSL (Extensible Style Sheet Language)
SVG (Scalable Vector Graphics), 146
Syntax. *See also* document components
  compatibility with markup languages, 10
  defined, 2
  exercises, 37–39

namespaces, 86–89
online references, 36
overview, 20
parsers, 35
properties, CSS, 69–73
review questions, 36–37
rules, CSS, 69
schemas, 129–131
summary, 36
well-formed documents, 32–35
XHTML, 12

T

Tag delimiter characters, 25
Tags
content, 21
end, 21
HTML, 6, 12
start, 21, 34
user-defined, 12
XML, 10
Template, formatting, 123–125
Text, bolding, 2–3, 8–9
Text properties, 71
Title attribute, 107–109
Transforming documents, 119–127
Trees, 120
Type attribute, 106

U

Undirectional links, 104
Unicode Character Set, 26, 36
Unnamed character entities, 26
Unparsed entities, 25, 32
URIs (Uniform Resource Identifiers), 88–89
URLs (Uniform Resource Locators), 102

V

Validating parsers, 35, 44–48
Versioning, 145

W

W3C (World Wide Web Consortium)
HTML specifications, 5
pattern matching recommendations, 125
XLink specifications, 104
XML Schema Language recommendations, 61
XML specifications, 9, 16, 17, 36
WAP (Wireless Application Protocol), 146
Web browsers
Browser XML Display Chart online, 17
client programs, 6
defined, 4
HTML, 5–6, 12
XHTML, 12
XLink, 104
Web-DAV (Distributed Authoring and Versioning on the Web), 145
Well-formed documents
attributes, 33
DTDs, 59
nesting, 33
online references, 36
overlapping, 33
parent and child elements, 33
start tags, 34
strings, 34
Windows, 2, 4, 8
Wireless Application Protocol (WAP), 146
WordPerfect, 4
World Wide Web Consortium (W3C). *See* W3C (World Wide Web Consortium)

X

XHTML (Extensible Hypertext Markup Language), 12, 147
XLink, 104
XML Industry Portal, 17
XML overview
benefits, 10
definition of XML, 2
document creation, 13–16
exercises, 17, 19
future developments, 150, 152
HTML vs., 11–12
introduction, 1
need for, 9–11
online references, 17, 18, 36, 151–152
review questions, 17, 19
summary, 17
XML programming. *See* programming, with XML
XML Query Language(XQuery), 144–145
XMLDOM, 138–142
XPath, 113
XPointer, 113
XQuery (XML Query Language), 144–145
XSL (Extensible Style Sheet Language)
CSS and, 68, 79, 80
exercises, 133–134
importance of, 118
online references, 132
overview, 117–119
review questions, 133
summary, 132
transforming XML to HTML, 122–127
XSLT, 119–127
XSL-FO (XSL Formatting Objects), 119